The Mindful Relationship

the **mindful relationship**

Easy Exercises to Make Mindfulness a Daily Relationship Practice

Lauren Korshak, LMFT

ROCKRIDGE PRESS

Interior and Cover Designer: Jami Splitter

Art Manager: Sue Smith

Editor: Claire Yee

Production Editor: Mia Moran

Illustration: Maram/Shutterstock

Author Photo courtesy of Marilyn Isaac

ISBN: Print 978-1- 64152-651-7 | eBook 978-1- 64152-652-4

This book is dedicated to my clients.
Thank you for trusting me to guide you,
for knowing your value
and the worth of your relationships,
for believing in transformation,
and for your courage.
I believe in you.

And to my parents, Louise and Stuart,
for their wise guidance and support;
after 49 years of marriage,
they are still visibly in love.

contents

Love said to me,
there is nothing that is not me.
be silent.

I will whisper secrets in your ear
just nod yes
and be silent.

—RUMI

Introduction

WELCOME

Rumi knew the power of stillness. I don't know how he knew, whether through meditation or an innate spiritual inclination, but he understood how inner quiet can transform love. Rumi knew that the universal yearning for greater love and connection starts with cultivating deep stillness in ourselves.

You probably chose this book with some awareness of the power of stillness and mindfulness to transform your life. Maybe you already have your own mindfulness practice but want to find a way to share it with your partner; perhaps you've noticed unhelpful patterns in your relationship and believe mindfulness could help unravel them. Maybe you want to feel more desired, seen, and loved in your partnership. Whatever your reasons, you'll find that the practices in this book have the power to change the dynamics of your relationship for the better.

Over the last decade in my work as a therapist, I have seen firsthand the power of mindfulness to transform couples' relationships from reactive roller coasters to respectful, loving partnerships. In this book, I provide the foundational knowledge and skills you need to weave mindfulness, compassion, communication skills, and gratitude seamlessly into your relationship so that you, too, can experience this power.

Intimate relationships are arguably the most complex daily challenge we face and, simultaneously, the main determinant of our happiness and quality of life. It's commonly said that the happiest people are those in good romantic relationships, the next happiest are people who are not in romantic relationships, and the least happy are people in bad relationships. Research shows that the quality of our relationships impacts our health and happiness far more than simply having a relationship; in other words, just partnering up isn't going to make you happy in and of itself. For this reason, reading this book and making time for these practices is one of the best things you can do to improve your relationship and quality of life.

This book isn't a "quick fix" but a journey toward seeing yourself, your relationship, and your partner clearly, without projections and judgments. This journey asks you to be honest with yourself as you face unconscious patterns, open up to your partner, and courageously meet challenges in new ways. If you commit to the practices outlined in this book, the grip of painful patterns, behaviors, and mindsets will start to loosen, and in their place, the seeds of wisdom, courage, self-knowledge, and intimacy will begin to sprout. I look forward to helping guide you on this journey.

HOW TO USE THIS BOOK

This book contains practical suggestions, psychotherapy techniques, and mindfulness practices designed to address the most common relationship challenges. You'll notice that each chapter is peppered with practice exercises that help you more fully integrate the chapter concepts. Additionally, there is a list of exercises at the back of the book, organized by chapter, so you can easily find your way back to practices you want to revisit as you continue working through the book.

This book is not about the achievement of a specific outcome but about the ongoing process and practice of growth. As such, set manageable expectations for yourself and your partner and give yourself permission to take breaks to support your motivation to keep practicing!

To support this process, I suggest you have the following:

◈ A journal: Research shows that writing down your thoughts supports integration and learning. Choose a journal that makes you happy when you look at it! Each partner should have their own journal.

◈ A timer: Most meditation exercises are timed. If you use your smartphone, find a soothing alert tone. The app Insight Timer, for example, has a meditation bell sound.

◈ Meditation props: A good meditation cushion, meditation bench, or straight-back chair will help support your practice.

◈ Practice place: A consistent place in your home where distractions are minimized can "cue" you for meditation. Make the ambience of your space relaxing and supportive with candles, an essential oil diffuser, and meaningful objects that remind you of your practice intentions.

◈ A therapist (possibly): Because these exercises are experiential, they may activate emotional responses. If you feel overwhelmed or want to deepen your experience, you may benefit from the support of a qualified psychotherapist trained in mindfulness or somatic (body-oriented) approaches.

A NOTE ON POSTURE: When doing the meditative practices, sit comfortably with a straight, long spine or lie down if that's what the exercise instructs. If meditation is new to you, experiment with different props and positions to see what best supports your posture.

GETTING STARTED

The benefits of this book come from consistent practice, which requires planning. After you've purchased your journals, sit with your partner, review the layout of this book, and schedule daily or weekly practice sessions. I recommend each partner spend 15 to 20 minutes (or more) daily on solo practices and work together for longer sessions on joint practices at least two to three times per week. In most cases, you can do the solo practices alongside each other if your schedules allow.

For pacing, ideally you would spend two to three months on each part (or six to nine months on the whole book), but tailor this to your unique relationship needs. Individually or as a couple, read a chapter over the course of one to two weeks, practicing the exercises as you go. When you reach the chapters focused on putting your practices to work, spend some extra time repeating the practices you've done before moving on to the next part. But again, modify the pace to suit your lifestyle and time constraints—this is one of the things you and your partner should figure out together.

You may choose to skip ahead if you'd like to focus on a specific skill or challenge; however, since the chapters build upon one another, I encourage you to follow the order of the book as much as possible.

You'll notice this book is sprinkled with examples of real couples to help illuminate the concepts I discuss. Please note that their names and identifying information have been changed to protect their privacy.

Okay, let's take a deep breath and begin!

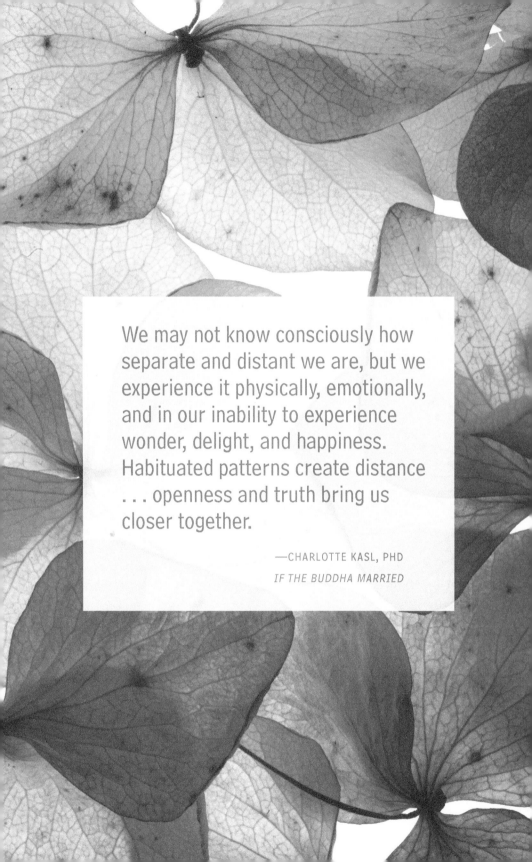

We may not know consciously how separate and distant we are, but we experience it physically, emotionally, and in our inability to experience wonder, delight, and happiness. Habituated patterns create distance . . . openness and truth bring us closer together.

—CHARLOTTE KASL, PHD
IF THE BUDDHA MARRIED

PART ONE

Managing Conflict

THE CHALLENGE

Conflict is a natural part of any relationship. Couples often believe they shouldn't have conflict or would prefer not to "rock the boat." Such beliefs lead to avoiding conflict and each other, weakening the couple's bond and their intimacy. Other times, couples are not afraid of conflict but may have unhealthy patterns of communicating their differences or may be more invested in "being right" than resolving conflict.

Every difficult moment, conflict, and rupture in a relationship is an opportunity to deepen intimacy and strengthen the relationship if couples can face these moments with mindfulness, awareness, integrity, and respect. Resolving conflict successfully involves the ability to tend to one's own needs and feelings, and healthy conflict resolution actually leads to a healthy sense of interdependence and intimacy.

Mandy and Jamal came to therapy to better resolve conflict. In one session, Mandy recounted an unresolved fight from earlier that week when the couple was moving their furniture into a smaller apartment. One day, Mandy told Jamal that the living room (which was stockpiled with extra furniture) looked "so crowded." Before she could finish her sentence, Jamal interrupted to explain that he "knew from the look on her face" that Mandy was going to complain "before she even opened her mouth."

As Jamal spoke in the therapy session, his breathing accelerated, and his voice got louder. Mandy began arguing with him, and the conflict reemerged in the present moment.

THE REMEDY

The story I just shared illuminates the pivotal moment when a couple can either reenact their conflict cycles or pivot toward more intimacy through *present moment awareness*.

Present moment awareness is a foundational mindfulness tool that requires nonjudgmental witnessing of thoughts, emotions, feelings, and actions. By witnessing and observing sensations, feelings, and thoughts in the present moment, each partner can respond to the moment rather than react to their story about the situation or their partner. This moment of pause and reflection allows each person a choice in how to respond, and offers couples a way out of cycles of hurt, blame, or reactivity.

During that session, Jamal and Mandy practiced stopping and observing their body sensations and emotions mid-conflict. As Jamal slowed down his reaction with mindfulness, he noticed that underneath his frustration at Mandy, he felt overwhelmed about the move, and when Mandy expressed her concern, he felt pressure to "fix the problem," which led him to react defensively. As Jamal became mindful of his feelings, his story about Mandy receded and his focus shifted to expressing rather than defending himself. Mandy sighed in relief and shared that she felt more warmth toward Jamal and a sense of "being in it together." She said she would try to express her own feelings directly next time rather than criticizing the situation.

Our refuge is in being exactly where we are . . . being the compassionate witness to our panic and fear—not judging it as good or bad, just accepting the *what is* of the moment.

—CHARLOTTE KASL, PHD
IF THE BUDDHA DATED

ONE

Present Moment Awareness

EVERYDAY MINDFULNESS

To experience the benefits of mindfulness in your relationship, you don't have to go on a silent retreat or sit cross-legged in a cave somewhere. You can experience the benefits simply by cultivating your attention and consistently practicing mindfulness skills. If you can abide by these two principles, I promise that you, your partner, and your relationship will benefit.

To feel truly free and happy in our relationships, we must be able to respond to life and the present moment as they are unfolding rather than acting from our habitual responses. Mindfulness helps us do this by teaching us to disengage from unhelpful thought patterns and to become nonjudgmental observers of our own bodies and minds. By cultivating nonjudgmental awareness, our patterns begin to shift. Studies show that when the mind is at rest, it will wander, but that when the mind wanders, people feel the least happy. Practicing mindfulness increases happiness by giving the mind a focus (such as the breath) and deactivating its wandering tendencies, even when we are not actively meditating.

In addition to promoting feelings of happiness, mindfulness has been proven to reduce stress, decrease emotional reactivity, strengthen focus and working memory, increase relationship satisfaction, improve communication, enhance sleep, hasten recovery from illness, prevent burnout, relieve depression, and improve overall mental health. If you picked up this book, you're probably familiar with some of these benefits. Still, you may be wondering, "What exactly is mindfulness, and how can I apply it to my relationship?"

Mindfulness is simply the practice of bringing open, curious, nonjudgmental awareness to the present moment with willingness to accept and be with what is. The following exercises will help you practice this kind of awareness in your relationship in daily life so that you can respond to your partner with more self-awareness, authenticity, and flexibility.

Practice: BREATH AWARENESS

Breath awareness is a foundational tool of mindfulness. In mindfulness practice, the mind is usually focused on an "anchor" (a word, phrase, or body process upon which we rest our attention). In this exercise, the breath will be your anchor. Breath awareness allows you to practice present moment awareness anytime and anywhere, and to connect with your body's feelings, sensations, and natural rhythm. Aim to practice for 5 minutes at first, working up to 20 minutes over time. You can practice solo or alongside your partner.

1. Set a timer. Sit comfortably with a long, straight spine. Breathe normally. Close your eyes, and bring your awareness and attention to where the air enters your nose.

2. Let your awareness follow your inhalation into your lungs and belly, and follow your exhalation as the air leaves your belly and lungs and exits your nose.

3. Observe and follow your breath's natural rhythm without judging it or trying to change it. You may notice the rhythm is fast and shallow, or slow and labored.

4. Notice where in your body the breath goes; perhaps it moves into your chest, lungs, back, or lower belly.

5. If your mind wanders to thoughts or worries or you notice emotions like sadness or frustration, acknowledge each thought or feeling by labeling it "thought," "sadness," or "frustration," and gently guide your awareness back to the breath.

6. When the timer rings, open your eyes and take a moment to notice how you feel in your body.

Repeat this breath awareness practice daily this week, and take mindful pauses throughout your day to notice your breath's natural rhythm. Try using the practice during tense conversations, meetings, or before bed with your partner. In your journal, jot down how it felt to use breath awareness in different settings.

Another way to build mindfulness into your relationship is to bring present moment awareness to daily activities. The next exercise focuses on mindful eating, because meals are a daily opportunity to connect and deepen our bond with our partners. Mindful eating also activates our pleasure centers and connects us with our bodies. Often we eat in reaction to time demands or to cope with difficult emotions. When we eat mindfully rather than reactively, we enhance our sense of satisfaction, pleasure, and connection.

Research shows that the average American spends only an hour and seven minutes daily eating food. However, if we spend this time mindfully, benefits abound, including decreased compulsive behavior, improved overall health, and even better digestion—all things that help us show up as more present partners.

Practice: A MINDFUL MEAL

With your partner, plan at least 30 minutes of silence during a meal to experience a deep level of connecting. Don't worry about "getting it right." Simply focus on being receptive to your sensory experience.

1. Choose a meal with nourishing, pleasurable, healthy foods.

2. Light a candle, dim the lights, and arrange your food intentionally on your plate.

3. Sit down to eat, close your eyes, and take three breaths: On the first exhale, breathe out worries about the past; on the second,

breathe out thoughts of the future; and on the third, embrace the present moment.

4. Inhale the smell of the food with several long, deep breaths. Notice if you start to salivate or where you feel anticipation in your body.

5. Listen to the sounds around you until you feel calm, relaxed, and less reactive to any noise.

6. Gently open your eyes and look at what you are about to eat; receive the food with your eyes.

7. Slowly start eating, noticing the texture of the food on your lips and tongue. Take your time, perhaps even holding the food in your mouth for a moment.

8. Notice different flavor profiles as if tasting this food for the first time.

9. As you swallow, sense the food moving down your throat and into your belly, and feel or imagine the digestion process beginning.

10. Let your attention move between your senses. If your mind wanders to thoughts of the past or future, pause, put your fork down, and re-center by taking three breaths.

When you feel pleasantly full, take a moment to appreciate your body, your senses, and the nourishing food. Discuss the experience with your partner, noting equally parts of the exercise that felt good and parts that felt challenging.

Now we will apply some of these mindful awareness skills you've practiced to nonjudgmental observation of yourself in daily life.

MINDFUL AWARENESS OF SELF

Many of the daily actions we take are done on autopilot. We wash dishes, take showers, type, eat, drive, and do a multitude of other things without any mindful attentiveness. When we start to mindfully observe our actions and their accompanying thoughts, emotions, and sensations, we deepen self-awareness. The quality of the relationship we develop with ourselves serves as a foundation for the quality of the relationship we can cultivate with our partners. The exercises here draw from body-based mindfulness practices to facilitate greater intimacy with ourselves and thereby with our partners.

The body scan is a traditional mindfulness practice in which we practice "being with" and physically experiencing each part of our body. This builds our ability to sense and feel inwardly, which strengthens the body-mind connection and teaches us to calm our nervous systems in times of stress or conflict.

Practice: BODY SCAN

The body scan should take 10 to 20 minutes. You can take turns reading aloud and guiding each other through the meditation (always guide more slowly than you think), or record the instructions and do the scan as you listen, either together or individually. You can also find a guided body scan under "Meditations" on my website, LaurenKorshakMFT.com.

1. Sit or lie on your back with your spine straight, hands at your sides, and feet shoulder-width apart (use a pillow under your head and knees for support if you are lying down).

2. Take several nourishing deep breaths, in through your nose and out through your mouth, and gently close your eyes.

3. Starting at the crown of your head, scan each part of your body from the inside out with your awareness. Observe qualities and areas of tension in the body with nonjudgmental awareness as you move through each part—that is, without resistance or trying to change anything (e.g., comfort, discomfort, shoulder tension, etc.).

4. Slowly and thoroughly move down through each part of the body—attending to the face, sides and back of the head, jaw, neck, shoulders, arms, hands, fingertips, chest, stomach, midback, lower back, lower belly, hips, pelvis, tops of the legs, knees, lower legs,

ankles, and feet—until you reach your toes. (If helpful, you can visualize a ball of white light slowly moving down your body.)

5. If your mind wanders, bring your attention back to the scan.

6. When you're ready, gently open your eyes, stretch, and notice how your body feels.

After the scan, you may find that you feel more relaxed and in touch with your body. I recommend practicing the body scan daily.

You may further develop this nonjudgmental awareness through cultivating "beginner's mind"—a spirit of openness, eagerness, and childlike curiosity. This phrase, often used in mindfulness practice, conflicts with achievement-oriented cultural values that drive us to be adept in every aspect of our lives. We are often encouraged to become experts in our fields, to "fake it till you make it," and are rewarded with praise when we act decisively, pretend to know, and check off boxes on to-do lists.

In striving to be the best at achieving things, we cut ourselves off from the tender, childlike part of us. Tolerating ambiguity is an essential aspect of discerning our feelings and relating to our partners, and honoring this ambiguity leads to more clarity and deeper intimacy.

As a child raised in a patriarchal household, my client Jamal was taught to believe his worth was defined by making the "right" decisions for his family as the "man of the house." This led Jamal to avoid expressing anything uncertain or to do anything he did not feel proficient in, such as sharing emotions. In his relationship with Mandy, Jamal's desire to avoid fights stemmed from his belief that he was "not good at emotions." In our sessions, he challenged this belief and embraced beginner's mind by exploring and sharing his feelings. Mandy practiced receiving him with the curiosity and openness of beginner's mind rather than defaulting to her usual fearful responses. Both partners started to feel closer as they began to see each other with fresh eyes and respond more creatively and spontaneously to each other.

The following exercise is a practice in attuning to our bodies and sensory experience with a beginner's mind. It may be hard at first to identify sensations, but in true beginner's fashion, you will get better with practice!

This exercise can also be used to regulate anxiety and calm the nervous system in times of distress.

Practice: CULTIVATING BEGINNER'S MIND

This solo exercise should take about 10 minutes. It provides the foundation for the future exercises you'll do with your partner.

1. Sit comfortably.

2. Notice what emotion you feel and how strongly you feel it on a scale of 1 to 10.

3. Inhale deeply. Soften and close your eyes as you exhale.

4. Name the first three internal sensations you notice (e.g., butterflies in stomach, pain in left wrist, tightness in shoulders).

5. Softly open your eyes. Name the first three external sights, sounds, or smells you notice (e.g., the call of birds, the texture of the walls, the clock, the scent of your laundry detergent).

6. Repeat steps 2 through 4 at least three times. The objects or sensations you name can be the same or different each time—simply follow where your attention is drawn.

7. When complete, notice how you feel in your body and how strongly feel your initial emotion now. Note whether your initial emotion shifted in intensity.

In your journal, jot down any takeaways about how you felt before and after the exercise.

When we are more intimate with the internal sensations, thoughts, and feelings that comprise our inner landscape, we can better understand ourselves and communicate our feelings to our partners—creating a foundation for connection and deeper relating.

MINDFUL AWARENESS OF (SIGNIFICANT) OTHERS

Relationships are a dance in balancing closeness and autonomy. A healthy relationship is one in which both partners feel close and connected, while also maintaining a sense of freedom and independence. Sometimes we strive so hard to create intimacy that we lose ourselves. Alternatively, we can struggle so much for independence that we end up lonely and disconnected from our partners. In long-term relationships, each partner must balance tending to their individual needs with tending to the needs of their partner.

In my practice, I draw on a mindful movement practice known as Authentic Movement, which begins as a two-person practice in which one person (the witness) silently witnesses the movements of the other (the mover) using their senses to perceive the other person's thoughts, feelings, movements, and sensations. This practice allows the mover and witness to see, feel, and attune more deeply to their own inner world and that of the other, beneath the everyday external trappings of language and physical appearance. One of many gifts of this practice is that the witness's presence allows the mover to be exactly as they are in each moment, giving the mover the freedom to dance at the scary edge of vulnerability.

I find this practice of witnessing a great metaphor for building intimacy in couples. Often, when couples come to me, one or both partners complain that they don't get their individual needs met because they are so focused on their partner's needs.

Rhett and Marisol came to counseling to improve their relationship, noting their tendencies to be "a little codependent and do everything together most of the time" and, alternatively, "to be really awful to each other when stressed." They recounted a small fight in which Rhett snapped at Marisol that he didn't want to hear about her theory of why a museum closed early that day. In discussing the fight in the session, Marisol shared that she felt hurt because she'd spent months listening to Rhett talk about which bike he wanted to buy, and he didn't show her the same courtesy.

Rhett reflected that on that day he had had a headache and was experiencing work stress that had led him to snap at Marisol. He was unable to attune to himself in that moment, let alone recognize that what Marisol cared about was being seen by her partner, not the museum. Marisol reflected that she needed to work on recognizing her limits so that she didn't end up growing resentful. In sessions, Rhett and Marisol worked on slowing down and being mindful and responsive to their own feelings, as well as each other's body language, tone, and feelings, rather than simply reacting to each other from a place of stress.

One way to practice attuning to your partner is to do the previous "Cultivating Beginner's Mind" practice (see page 11) in the presence of each other, which is the focus of the next exercise. You will be attending to your own body while compassionately witnessing your partner attending to theirs.

Practice: ATTUNING TO OUR PARTNERS (OR "BAE MEDITATION")

This joint exercise, so titled by one of my clients, should take about 20 minutes, or 10 minutes per turn. Sit comfortably facing each other, and take turns guiding each other by reading the steps aloud. When you guide, bring your awareness to your partner's words and body language.

1. Take a deep breath, and slowly release it.

2. Name aloud the emotion you are feeling and how strongly you feel it on a scale of 1 to 10.

3. On your next exhale, allow your eyes to close.

4. Name aloud the first three internal sensations you notice.

5. Softly open your eyes. Name aloud the first three external sights, sounds, or smells you notice. (*Guide your partner through the steps at least two more times.*)

6. Open your eyes. Describe how you feel in your body and how strongly on a scale of 1 to 10 you now feel the emotion you named in step 2.

Share with your partner how it felt to guide this exercise and witness your partner's experience. Discuss how it felt to be witnessed. The following "Go Deeper" exercise will help you explore this exercise more in depth.

GO DEEPER
Reflecting on Attunement

Mindfulness exercises are more powerful when we can integrate them into our daily lives with reflection and regular practice. Writing facilitates deeper self-reflection, awareness, and insight. In your journal, respond to the following prompts; do not be afraid to go off topic.

◈ How did it feel to tune in to myself in the "Cultivating Beginner's Mind" practice on page 11?

◈ How did it change when I did the same exercise in the presence of my partner?

◈ What was it like to guide my partner through the process?

◈ How did it feel to attune to my partner?

◈ What can I do daily to more deeply attune to myself? To my partner?

BRINGING AWARENESS TO YOUR RELATIONSHIP

In addition to our individual needs and our partners' needs, our relationships *themselves* have needs, expectations, and agreements that require our attention. Like a garden, a relationship requires ongoing care, nurturing, and supportive conditions for trust and intimacy to flourish. If the needs of the relationship are neglected, each individual may feel like the relationship is lifeless, lackluster, or even toxic. If the relationship is properly tended, it becomes a sacred space where individuals can feel safe to take risks, grow, explore, and rely on each other in new ways.

So, how do you tend to your relationship? You plant seeds of intention (how you would like to be and what you value as a couple) and tend to them with mindfulness, honesty, communication, gratitude, forgiveness, kindness, and compassion just as you would give your garden the water, sunlight, air, and soil it needs to thrive.

Kalia and Shane are a couple in their early forties who came to therapy to remedy a sense of disconnection in their 10-year relationship. Although each partner was thriving in their life and career, their once passionate relationship had started feeling dull.

To nurture their relationship, Kalia and Shane began a daily heart meditation practice and reading a spiritual book together. These practices led to feelings of connection, new conversations, and collaborative, creative career events that they incorporated into their new practices. The couple started feeling more connected intellectually, spiritually, and emotionally; however, the relationship was still sexually and romantically unsatisfying. The couple realized they missed reveling in each other's company, so they began a ritual of monthly date nights. Within several months, they noticed the seeds of playfulness, curiosity, and passion start to sprout again.

Like Kalia and Shane, we may be so immersed in our lives that we don't notice at first that we feel separate or distant from our partners. However, on a physical and emotional level, our bodies register this disconnection, and this inhibits our ability to feel the wonder, delight, and happiness available in our relationship.

When we generate positive feelings like loving-kindness or joy, our brain waves synchronize with the activity of our heart, and we are able to come into what the HeartMath organization has coined "a state of coherence," a physiological state characterized by increased harmony in our mental, emotional, and physiological processes that leads to feelings of peace, ease, and well-being. In a state of coherence, we experience greater emotional stability, increased mental clarity, and improved cognitive function. When we connect with our partners in a loving way, this state is heightened as our heart rhythms and biochemistries synchronize with each other's. The following meditation is one Kalia and Shane used to cultivate these feelings of well-being.

Practice: HEART MEDITATION

This joint meditation will take about 20 minutes for practice and discussion.

1. Sit next to your partner, and set a timer for 10 to 15 minutes.

2. Close your eyes and tune in to your heartbeat. If you have trouble, simply intend to feel your heart's rhythm.

3. If your attention drifts to thoughts, sounds, or feelings, label these: "thought," "sound," "love," "anger," etc., as if you are greeting a visitor, and then return your attention to your heartbeat.

4. Bring to mind a joyful memory of a time with your partner. Connect with the feelings of joy and love in your heart.

5. Place your hand in the space between you and your partner. When you feel your partner's hand arrive, gently hold hands. Notice if your heartbeat responds to the touch of your partner's hand.

6. Begin alternating your awareness between your own heartbeat and your partner's hand. As you inhale, notice your heartbeat. As you exhale, pay attention to the sensation of your partner's hand in yours. You may sense a gentle pulsing or feel the temperature or texture of their hand.

7. When the timer rings, take a moment to observe how you feel and how connected you feel to your partner.

Make loving eye contact and smile at your partner when the exercise concludes. If it feels right, hug and notice your heartbeat and your partner's heartbeat. Spend a few moments sharing your experience with each other.

To flourish, relationships require protected time to simply enjoy each other's company and get to know each other as you are now. Remember the excitement of dating, the unfamiliarity of the new person, and the unknown of how your relationship would unfold? The following exercise is intended to re-create some of that excitement and passion.

Practice: PLAN A MINDFUL DATE

This joint exercise should take about 30 minutes. Remove distractions, light a candle, and grab your journals and calendars.

1. Agree to create a regular date night. Decide on the frequency (I recommend monthly) and how you will alternate who is planning (I recommend every other date night be planned by one partner and presented as a surprise to the other).

2. Schedule the time in your calendars.

3. Discuss planning guidelines (e.g., if finances are an issue, create a budget; if childcare is a consideration, discuss who will handle those arrangements each time).

4. Create a shared wish list. In your journals, list five date wishes that would ignite passion and connection in your relationship. Take turns discussing your wishes and add these to a shared list (you may use a shared phone note or document, or a couples app like Between). Consider hobbies, romantic ideas, or activities that reflect you as a couple (e.g., exercising, eating out, reading, classes, vacations, or skydiving). The list should stimulate creativity, discovery, and understanding of each other.

5. Decide who will plan the first date. When it's your turn to plan, make it a mindful activity rather than another rushed to-do list item.

6. Get ready for your first mindful date night!

Mindfully tending to your relationship can enhance passion by helping you see each other in new ways. It can also create a positive emotional reservoir you can draw upon in difficult moments.

Wrap-Up

◈ Relationship patterns can shift through nonjudgmental awareness of them.

◈ Breath awareness and paying attention to our senses at a meal are great ways to bring everyday mindfulness to our relationship.

◈ Cultivating beginner's mind allows us to become more responsive, present, intimate, and aware in our relationship.

◈ By attuning to ourselves, we can better attune to our partner's needs and feelings.

◈ A relationship is an entity that needs nurturing. We can tend to our relationship with practices and rituals like meditation and date nights.

Owning our story can be hard but not nearly as difficult as spending our lives running from it. Embracing our vulnerabilities is risky but not nearly as dangerous as giving up on love and belonging and joy . . . Only when we are brave enough to explore the darkness will we discover the infinite power of our light.

—BRENÉ BROWN
THE GIFTS OF IMPERFECTION

TWO

Getting Unstuck from Your Stories

HOW STORIES HELP AND HURT

The human mind is a master storyteller and for good reason: Stories are adaptive and entertaining. They help us make sense of complexity and feel empathy, and they provide cultural scripts for human interactions. From ancient myths and religious texts to theater, movies, and social media, stories draw us in and engage us.

However, our innate ability to generate stories can backfire and cause suffering when we accept stories we have created about ourselves and our lives as factually true. Stories that we may have generated in early childhood or in response to difficult or traumatic experiences can distort our perception of our current reality. Acceptance and Commitment Therapy (ACT) refers to this tendency to believe our thoughts and stories as "cognitive fusion." When we "fuse" with our stories, we're likely to react to our thoughts rather than respond to the present moment as it is unfolding. This often leads us to behave in problematic ways.

For example, being fused with a belief that your partner never listens to you may lead you to avoid interactions and conversations with your partner by burying yourself in social media, despite the fact that connection and intimacy are important to you. Other stories we create may be about our identities ("I am a survivor"), our past or future ("I've always failed" or "Everyone will leave me"), our judgments ("Feeling sad is unbearable" or "She's lazy"), or rules ("Sharing feelings is weak" or "I shouldn't care about this").

When we find ourselves ruminating, withdrawing, blaming, criticizing ourselves or others, or imposing rules and "shoulds," we are usually reacting to a story rather than what's happening in the present moment. This is limiting to us and those around us. Mindfulness teaches us to notice our stories, so we can hold them more loosely, allowing us to feel less reactive and our partners to feel more freedom in our presence.

Early in their courtship, Muhammed asked Laleh on many dates, but she often had to reschedule, leaving Muhammed feeling rejected. He stopped asking in favor of a more unplanned approach. Years later in counseling, Laleh expressed her need for Muhammed to take more initiative. Muhammed explained that, in the back of his mind, he was afraid to plan dates because he knew Laleh would just cancel them. Once Muhammed named his story, Laleh was able to reassure him that she wouldn't cancel, and the old story that had been controlling Muhammed's behavior lost some of its power. And as Muhammed started to plan more dates, Laleh's story that Muhammed "never took initiative" started to lose its hold on her.

In ACT, when we take a step back from our thoughts and view them more objectively, it's called "cognitive defusion." You probably practice this sometimes without even realizing it. Defusion strategies you may already use include laughing about a difficult situation (think parodies, stand-up comedy, or political comics) or reframing (shifting our focus). When we defuse from our thoughts, we access greater choice and freedom in how we respond to a situation. In the previous example, Muhammed was able to shift his reaction from avoidance to more active engagement with his wife. This led to Laleh feeling happier and more connected to Muhammed, which led to greater intimacy in their relationship.

This next mindfulness practice is a simple and effective visualization technique that will help you begin to defuse from your stories.

This short meditation can be done solo or alongside your partner.

1. Set a timer for 5 to 7 minutes.

2. Sit comfortably, and close your eyes. Take several slow breaths, noticing sensations, feelings, and thoughts without judgment.

3. Imagine a stream flowing in front of you. See the water traveling by and leaves from nearby trees falling into the water and floating downstream.

4. Call to mind a specific situation or story that is troubling you. (If nothing particular comes to mind, just notice thoughts that arise.)

5. Bring your awareness to your thoughts. Allow them to take a shape or form into sentences.

6. Take each thought, place it on a leaf, and watch it float downstream. (If you think in images or are only aware of body sensations, place those on the leaves.)

7. If repeating thoughts, worries, memories, or judgments such as "This isn't working" arise, place them on a leaf, too, and let them float away.

8. When the timer rings, gently open your eyes, and notice how you feel in your body.

Take a few moments to jot down any insights in your journal. Aim to practice this meditation daily.

In addition to mindfulness practices, cultivating humor and present-moment responsiveness help cultivate a sense of distance from our stories. The following exercise is derived from an improv game and helps us detach from our stories in a playful, more interactive way.

Practice: YES-NO

This joint exercise should take about 20 minutes, but you can continue beyond that if you choose. Each partner takes a turn being the storyteller.

1. Choose a story you have about yourself or your partner.

2. As one partner tells the story, the other partner will interject periodically by saying "no" to change the direction of the story or "yes" to keep it on course.

3. The storytelling partner will continue telling the story following the same storyline whenever the listener says "yes," but they must immediately switch the storyline by restating the last statement when the listener says "no." Here's an example:

You: "I didn't follow through today, and I feel terrible about myself . . ."

Partner: "No."

You: "I'm actually feeling pleased with myself . . ."

Partner: "Yes."

You: "So I decided I would reward myself and take a bubble bath . . ."

Partner: "No."

You: "So I decided I wouldn't reward myself, I would go running . . ."

Have fun with each other and your "yeses" and "nos" in this exercise. Let them be guided by impulse, rather than ideas of right and wrong. Enjoy the creative and empowering aspect of your ability to create and recreate stories! When we are less attached to our stories, we are more able to define the kind of life we want to live.

When we're reactive to our stories, we define our actions through reactions like avoidance, resistance, or passive acceptance rather than acting from an authentic place. When we defuse from our stories, we're free to let our actions be guided by our most important values. In ACT, values represent our most deeply held beliefs and the things that give our lives meaning. Connectedness, honesty, or compassion are examples of values people might hold for their relationships. In your relationship, values help you embody the kind of partner you want to be and define what you stand for. Values guide, motivate, and inspire us to move toward what is important to us.

GO DEEPER

Your Best Life

What values guide you and your relationship? To explore this, spend 10 minutes, solo or jointly, on the following exercise.

1. Sit comfortably with your eyes closed, and imagine you and your partner in old age reflecting on your life together. Imagine feeling a deep sense of ease, joy, and contentment.

2. Open your eyes, and write a list of all the values or qualities reflected in this vision (e.g., generosity, loyalty, courage, creativity, growth, intimacy, depth, passion, exploration).

3. Next to each item, rate how much you currently live in accordance with this value on a scale of 1 to 10. For example, if you feel you don't have much intimacy in your daily life, you might score it a 2 or 3, or if you feel highly creative at work, you might score it a 9 or 10.

Defining our life by our values means that we do more than simply state our values; we align our behaviors with them. Reflect on any obstacles to fulfilling these values and how you can bring them more into your life right now.

STORIES ABOUT YOURSELF

As master storytellers, we can't help but use our storytelling powers on ourselves. We have stories about the kind of person we are ("I'm a good person"), what we're good at ("I make an amazing blueberry pie"), and what we're not good at ("I'm terrible at communicating"). But how true are these stories? And more important, how useful is it for us to cling to them? Many of our stories reflect ideas we may have formed as far back as childhood and lead us to identify with a rigid idea of ourselves that may not be serving us anymore.

Rose and Malik have been together since high school. Their relationship became lackluster as they devoted themselves to childrearing and their careers at the expense of their individual pursuits and values. One of the challenges in their relationship was Rose's depression and the financial stress on the relationship of Rose not working. She loved to bake and made beautifully decorated cakes for her friends and family. Her loved ones encouraged her to start a business, but Rose had a story that she was "not a businesswoman." As she began facing the underlying fear of failure that drove her story, Rose was able to defuse from her story and follow her heart and values. She enrolled in a women's business support program and started her bakery, which more than eight years later is now a successful high-end bakery.

By choosing to confront rather than believe her story, Rose began to show up in her relationship in a new way—with enthusiasm and a sense of fulfillment—and her newfound engagement with work eased the couple's financial stress.

The following exercise is designed to help you notice stories that may be influencing your life, so that you can begin to loosen their hold on you.

This joint exercise should take about 20 minutes and requires your journals.

1. In your journals, jot down a list of common phrases, beliefs, and stories you repeat to yourself and others about yourself. For example, if you repeatedly say, "I'm complicated," "I just don't do emotions," or "I'm a loner," write that down.

2. If you need to jog your memory, skim your journaling notes so far or old journals if you have them. Notice any repeated statements or beliefs.

3. Now, beneath each statement, write the following:

    - The approximate age at which the story began.
    - What your life would look like if you spent all your time acting in alignment with the story (e.g., if you spent all your time alone).
    - What your life could look like if this weren't true (e.g., if you spent most of your time with family or friends or got involved in a spiritual community). Brainstorm at least three possibilities for how life could look outside of your story.

4. Brainstorm action steps you can take that challenge each story (e.g., spend an entire day with people one day this week). Use SMART goals to make your goal specific, measurable, attainable, relevant, and time-bound. (If you are unfamiliar with SMART goals, see page 44.)

Share your insights with your partner. Continue developing your awareness by noticing stories and repeated phrases that arise this week. Add these to your list! Taking steps to confront our stories is challenging and courageous, but it deepens our self-awareness and liberates us to be more present in our relationships.

STORIES ABOUT YOUR PARTNER

Just as our stories limit our ability to see ourselves clearly, they inhibit our capacity to truly see our partners. We might not bother to ask our partners to empty the trash because we know (in our story) that they never do what we ask, leading us to resent them for the qualities we wrote into their story. Your partner can feel stories you have about them, just as you can feel your partner's stories about you. Living in reaction to stories about each other prevents us from responding as we are in the moment, impedes intimacy, and may cause us to feel angry, irritated, or repelled based on something that isn't real.

Ling and Trent are a recently married young couple that came to me to strengthen their new relationship. In times of difficulty and conflict, Ling became logical and solution-oriented, and Trent perceived her as cold and distant, leading him to withdraw, sulk, or lash out. This left Ling unsure of how to respond to Trent. Over time, Trent began to understand that his reaction was actually related to his story about Ling being cold and uncaring. Trent realized his reaction to his story (withdrawing, sulking) protected him from the possibility of being rejected but prevented him from clearly seeing the situation or feeling understood. As Trent began to share the fears, doubts, and anxieties underneath his story, he found that Ling responded with the love, compassion, and warmth he'd been seeking.

As we see with Trent and Ling's example, our stories protect us from facing difficult or uncomfortable emotions, but they can also undermine the closeness and intimacy we are seeking. If we can nonjudgmentally notice our stories about our partners and connect to the feelings beneath them, we can be more available to receive our partners as they are.

This solo journaling exercise should take about 15 minutes.

1. In your journal, make three columns.

2. In the first column, list thoughts and stories about your partner and your relationship. Note repetitive thoughts, phrases, or complaints you say repeatedly (e.g., "My partner never texts me back").

3. Look at each item on the list, and notice how each story impacts you. In the second column, note what emotions and physical sensations arise in reaction to each story (e.g., "anxious, angry, heart racing").

4. In the third column, write how you typically react when this story arises (e.g., "I text repeatedly and then give the silent treatment for an hour when they return").

Review each story and imagine different reasons your partner may have for acting the way they do. Imagine how it would feel to be the recipient of your stories, reactions, and behaviors. Allow yourself to feel some compassion for yourself and for your partner. Throughout the week, notice when thoughts and stories arise about your partner and how you feel and react in response. See if you can bring compassion to the situation, perhaps imagining breathing in a feeling of compassion for yourself and breathing out compassion for your partner.

Another way to detach from our stories is through understanding our partners' needs, strengths, and ways they prefer to receive love. In our sessions, Ling learned that Trent needed more warmth, words of affirmation, and physical touch when he felt triggered, and Trent learned that what he perceived as detachment was actually an expression of love.

"Love languages" are one tool for understanding these differences. Gary Chapman, author of *The Five Love Languages*, coined the term to describe five distinct ways humans express and experience love. He posits that people often give love in the way that they prefer to receive love, which is not always understood or received by their partner if they have a different love language. Learning each other's love languages can help you better see, understand, and appreciate each other. The five love languages are:

1. Words of affirmation

2. Gift giving

3. Quality time

4. Physical touch

5. Acts of service

Practice: LOVE LANGUAGES

This joint exercise calls for your journals. Spend about 15 minutes journaling and then about 15 minutes discussing.

1. In your journal, reflect on ways you prefer to receive love from your partner and ways in which your partner has expressed that they prefer to receive love from you.

2. List actions, words, and behaviors you would like your partner to use to express their love to you (e.g., "I love you" notes, gifts, cuddle time in the mornings, back rubs, or cooking for you).

3. Choose one item from this list you'd like your partner to focus on this week (perhaps one that would challenge a story you have about your partner).

4. Put your journals aside, and taking turns, express your appreciation to your partner for specific actions they took in the last several weeks that led you to feel connected, loved, and supported.

5. Make the request you chose in step 3 of your partner and describe how receiving that action would make you feel.

Better understanding our stories about ourselves and our partners allows space for us to respond to each other in ways that feel meaningful and aligned with our values rather than reactive and hotheaded. It is a skill that helps us see ways in which we may be creating stories about the relationship itself.

STORIES ABOUT YOUR RELATIONSHIP

In the same way you hold stories about yourself and your partner, your relationship itself carries a shared story (or stories) that can be limiting. When couples come to me for premarital counseling (as well as at other stages of their relationship), we engage in a structured assessment that reviews 15 major life dimensions. Couples either feel validated by results that reflect differences they already identified or feel surprised to discover challenges they couldn't see from the "inside." The assessment results give couples a fresh perspective of their relationship story as a whole and give each partner a window into how their partner's story about the relationship might differ from their own. Sometimes, couples have discussed aspects of their "couple story" before. For example, both partners may feel "we are just not a very health-oriented couple." Other times, couples may hold different stories (e.g., one partner may feel satisfied with their sex life, whereas the other may not).

Adam and Willa came to therapy for premarital counseling. Adam presented as confident, but his assessment test results told a different story. Adam scored low on assertiveness and self-confidence, and results showed that he felt Willa was the dominant partner. Willa was surprised because Adam appeared so confident, and Willa often talked about her feelings of insecurity. Looking beneath their shared "couple story" that Adam was confident and in control helped them more accurately see each other and understand their different experiences.

Exposing Adam's underlying feelings helped explain discrepancies in other aspects of the partnership—such as Adam's unhappiness with their sex life—and helped resolve financial difficulties where Adam hadn't voiced his financial needs and preferences. As Adam practiced asserting himself, Willa responded positively and made an effort to check in with him more often when making decisions. The couple moved toward a more balanced relationship in which Adam could safely express vulnerability, and Willa could recognize her own strength in addition to her insecurities.

So how do we break the hold of a shared story? How do we see our couple story clearly and show up from a place of authentic self-expression, mindfulness, vulnerability, and self-awareness? Like Willa and Adam, we notice where we are out of balance and we recalibrate, mindfully witnessing and accepting our partners as they are and asserting ourselves as we are.

Practice: STRENGTH AND GROWTH AREAS

This joint exercise is adapted from PREPARE/ENRICH premarital counseling tools, but it is useful at all stages of relationships. Plan to spend 15 minutes journaling and 15 minutes discussing, but adjust the time as needed.

1. In your journal, referring to the following list, jot down what you believe are the top three strength areas in your relationship. Then jot down the top three growth areas (i.e., areas that could be improved) in your relationship:

    - Communication
    - Conflict resolution
    - Partner style (personality) and habits
    - Financial management
    - Leisure activities
    - Sexuality and affection
    - Family and friends
    - Relationship roles
    - Children and parenting
    - Spiritual beliefs

2. Take turns sharing aloud one strength at a time, carefully describing what that domain means to you and why you consider it a strength.

3. Next, take turns sharing growth areas in the same fashion.

4. Discuss whether or not your partner's responses surprised you. Identify the areas where you are in agreement and where you may be in disagreement.

Once we better understand our couple story, it's time for the deeper work of showing up with our partners as we are. To deepen into intimacy, we must drop our stories and masks and simply be with each other, emotionally naked and vulnerable. This can be scary if we've been presenting our masked selves, as we may imagine our partners could reject us if we show them our real feelings.

The next practice is designed to help you open to the "feeling experience" that is deeper than your stories and connect with your partner from that place.

Practice: MEETING EACH OTHER AS WE ARE

This joint practice should take about 20 minutes (10 minutes for the meditation and 10 or so minutes for discussion). You can record the meditation ahead of time or simply remember the instructions.

1. Set a timer for 10 minutes.

2. Sit comfortably. Close your eyes and take several deep breaths.

3. Call to mind your first date.

4. Notice stories that arise (e.g., "He's so intelligent" or "She's so passionate"), as well as emotions and sensations in your body (e.g., excitement, tightness in your chest, butterflies in your stomach, etc.).

5. Allow memories of your relationship to arise, from the moment of your first meeting up until now—both good and bad (e.g., your first kiss, difficult experiences, anniversaries, a recent argument, etc.). As each memory arises, notice the stories, emotions, and sensations that come up.

6. Imagine opening your heart and accepting all the emotions that arise, from love and excitement to anxiety, fear, emptiness, shame, and guilt.

7. Continue breathing in these feelings with complete acceptance. Visualize breathing them into your heart, almost like clouds of smoke, and exhaling them as bright light.

8. When the timer rings, open your eyes as you exhale. Notice how you feel.

Take turns sharing your experience. Share memories that arose, stories that came up, and feelings and physical sensations you experienced. Sharing the feelings beneath the stories allows you to experience each other more deeply.

Unraveling our stories requires that we accept all the feelings underlying them, good and bad. When we can do this, we are free to see ourselves and our partners more clearly.

Wrap-Up

◈ Cognitive defusion, through mindfulness, humor, and other techniques, helps distance us from our stories, allowing us to respond to our partners as they are.

◈ A value is a way of being or believing that we hold important and that guides our lives. It's important not simply to state values but also to practice them.

◈ The stories we have are not always shared by our partners.

◈ We can move beneath our stories to see our partners more clearly through accepting and expressing our feelings.

We are what we repeatedly do. Excellence, then, is not an act, but a habit.

—WILL DURANT
THE STORY OF PHILOSOPHY

THREE

Putting Your Practices to Work

TURNING PRACTICE INTO HABIT

By now you have an idea of how to bring mindfulness into your relationship with your partner, but an idea is different from an ingrained habit! Like any other skill, mindfulness is more effective if it becomes a habitual part of your life. A habit is a specific, automatic pattern we develop in response to certain situations through consistent practice and repetition. With regular practice, your mindful responses will become automatic and not require as much energy and attention to enact.

There's a myth that it takes 21 days to build a habit; research shows that on average, it takes anywhere from two to eight months to create a lasting new behavior pattern. Therefore, integrating mindfulness into your life takes time, practice, commitment, and dedication. In this chapter, I provide suggestions to help incorporate these practices into your everyday life.

Two important tips to staying focused, committed, and effective in your habit formation practice are to set realistic expectations and to practice nonjudgment and self-compassion when you fall off track. Some weeks you may practice regularly, and some weeks you may falter. As soon as you notice you've strayed from your intention, simply return to your practice. Don't fall prey to the easy tendency to judge yourself for falling off track, as this kind of self-criticism is actually likely to decrease your motivation!

Planning

Mindful habit formation takes planning, especially in the beginning. Planning allows you to choose which skills are important to you and make time to practice them. Think of your plan as an anchor that you can return to when you wander away from your intention to practice. Decide together as a couple which techniques you want to prioritize for joint practice and decide which you want to prioritize for solo practice.

Research shows that the more we identify with the plans and goals we create, the more intrinsically motivated we are to initiate actions toward them, so choose techniques that you personally like as you follow these steps:

1. Review your journal notes from each exercise in this part of the book.

2. Highlight practices that felt powerful and inspiring and those that resonated with you. (Bonus points if you write which values underlie each practice you choose!)

3. Make a list of the top three joint exercises you'd like to practice in order of priority to discuss with your partner.

4. Make another list of the top three solo exercises you'd like to practice, and to the right of each solo practice, draw checkboxes so you can check them off as you complete them.

The next step in planning is deciding when and how often you will practice. Consider how you and your partner can reasonably fit these practices into your schedule. To do so:

1. Look at the recommended time for each practice on your solo list.

2. Determine when and how often you will fit this exercise into your calendar. Consider days and times when you will have natural breaks that would support consistent solo practice.

3. With your partner, review the exercises you each chose for joint practice. Then create a shared list of your top two to four exercises. Again, draw checkboxes to the right of each item so you can check them off as you complete them. (We'll use this list later in the chapter!)

Tracking Your Progress

Tracking progress is an important part of turning your mindfulness practice into a habit—and can even improve your mood! Directing awareness to little markers of progress has been shown to increase our sense of happiness, satisfaction, and motivation. As such, it's important to regularly pat ourselves (and our partners) on the back for the work we're doing and to acknowledge any relationship improvements we notice along the way.

The main avenues I recommend for tracking your progress are your calendar, your journal, and regular check-ins with your partner.

Calendar tracking: Use a month-at-a-glance wall calendar, a day planner, or your smartphone calendar to make short notes of practice activities, challenges, insights, and progress you notice each day. If possible, I recommend handwriting these notes. This gives you an overview of the work you are doing and an opportunity to commend yourself for your daily progress.

Journal tracking: In your journal, make detailed notes and reflections about your insights and any changes that result. Written reflection helps integrate thoughts and make new connections to what you're learning.

Partner check-ins: Regularly checking in with your partner to acknowledge the progress you have made individually and as a couple allows you to learn more about each other and gain insight you might not have uncovered alone. Check-ins also strengthen the positive feedback loop that will motivate you to keep practicing and help with habit formation. Check-ins can be weekly and/or daily rituals that involve reviewing your journals and tracking tools (bedtime or mealtimes are good times for this).

SETTING MUTUAL GOALS

Mindful, shared, values-based goal setting is essential to intentionally cocreating a mindful relationship.

Committed action is a concept in ACT that refers to "the development of larger and larger patterns of effective action linked to chosen values." Only through repeated engagement with practices that support our values can we can experience the life-changing benefits of bringing mindfulness to our relationship. Reading this book and having knowledge about mindfulness are important, but committed action is the key to seeing results. As with any commitment, we must continually recommit—when times are easy, when times are tough, when we feel inspired, and when we don't—to experience the gifts of our commitment. When you find yourself flagging, return to the mutual goals you share with your partner.

Now that we're on the same page . . . on to our practice plans!

Commitment to Solo Practice

Starting small is the key to implementing a new habit. In this exercise, you will commit to one daily solo practice using a commitment statement, which you will write in your journal. Make your commitment SMART:

- **S**pecific (include specific actions you want to accomplish)
- **M**easurable (something you can measure)
- **A**chievable (a goal you can actually meet)
- **R**elevant (connected to your values)
- **T**ime-bound (linked to a specific day, date, or time)

The following statement format is adapted from *The Five-Minute Journal*, published by Intelligent Change. Pick a practice from your solo list, and make a commitment to work it into your daily schedule this week. Write it down and share it with your partner, using the following prompts:

I, *(your name)*, commit to *(the practice)* at *(time)* for *(number)* days in a row, starting on *(day of the week)*. Taking this action is important to me because *(why it's important and how it connects to your values)*. I will set up myself for success by *(list what you will do)*:

Here's an example:

I, Jana Lee, commit to breath awareness at 7 a.m. for five days in a row, starting Monday. Taking this action is important to me because it supports my values of health and my relationship. I will set myself up for success by:

- *Placing my meditation cushion next to the bed*
- *Setting phone reminders*
- *Making nightly partner check-ins*

Commitment to Joint Practice

With your partner, pick another exercise that you can practice as a couple two or three times this week. Discuss how this exercise connects to your shared relationship values to increase your investment in this practice. Write a shared commitment statement in each of your journals.

We, *(your names)*, commit to *(the practice)* at least *(number)* day(s) this week, starting on *(day of the week)*. This is important to us because we *(why it's important)*.

We, Jana and Dan Lee, commit to the date night ritual at least one day this week, starting Monday. This is important to us because we value quality time.

GO DEEPER
Create Your Weekly Practice Schedule

Grab your partner and your calendars. Create a relaxing atmosphere, remove all distractions, and set a timer for 20 minutes. Spend this time mindfully adding the identified practices to your schedules.

Start by penciling in the practices you'll do as a couple. Decide how long to wait before you begin the next part of the book, and schedule accordingly. As you choose joint practices, think about how you might rearrange your schedules so that you can prioritize time to do these practices together. Next, pencil in the solo practices you will repeat over the next week or month.

Here are some tips to ensure your practices become habit:

◈ Set a consistent time.

◈ Pick a consistent place to practice.

◈ Set reminders.

◈ Use "cues" such as placing your meditation cushion nearby.

◈ Reward yourself for practicing (e.g., verbal appreciation, bubble baths, sparkling water, cuddle time, etc.).

◈ Be compassionate with yourself and each other. If you don't follow through, be kind to yourself and recommit!

CHECK-IN

As discussed, acknowledging progress is beneficial to your well-being and your relationship. Honest reflection also helps you assess growth, identify challenges, and recommit to your values when you've gotten off track. After a week, check in with yourself and your partner to reflect on how you have done with your goals this week.

How Did You Do?

Review your top six practices (solo and joint practice lists combined) and your commitment statements. Check off practices you completed, and notice which practices you didn't complete. Acknowledge yourself and your partner for every action you took, and take a moment to bask in that acknowledgment. Did you notice any differences in the quality of your relationship or your day? Would it be helpful to carry these same practices forward this week?

Also notice where you didn't meet your goals, and reflect on why this happened. Perhaps events outside your control got in the way, or maybe, as you reflect on the exercises, you realize you aren't motivated for the particular exercises you chose. Ask yourself if you would like to recommit to these practices in the coming week. Jot a few notes in your journal about how you can integrate some of these practices and why they are important to you as a way to keep yourself accountable. Readjust your calendar as needed!

Sticking with It

It's important to remember that building new habits can be challenging for a variety of reasons—life gets busy, we experience resistance, we forget, or we get sick. Getting off track does not mean that we have failed or that we are deficient. Instead, it is a reminder to take inventory of where we excelled (insert back pat here), where we were challenged (insert compassionate encouragement here), and where we simply forgot, avoided, or did not engage (recommit to values here). Rather than beat ourselves up, we can direct our energy toward asking, "What got in the way and why?" and work our plan from the awareness and understanding that arises when we answer that question for ourselves.

How you approach this book and the challenges you may encounter as you work through it are expressions of your unique values and learning styles as individuals—and as a couple. Each challenge is an opening to practice mindfulness, appreciation, and kindness for yourself, your partner, and your relationship.

Make sure to reward yourself and your partner with praise and appreciation for the hard work you are doing and the small challenges and progress you notice, rather than focusing on what you didn't do. In this way, you can nurture and nourish your seeds of motivation for practicing mindfulness.

Don't hesitate to enlist other couples, family members, friends, or a therapist or meditation teacher in this process. The more support and accountability structures you provide for yourself, the easier it will be to get back on track when your motivation is flagging.

Raise your words, not your voice.
It is rain that grows flowers, not
thunder.

—RUMI

PART TWO

Strengthening Communication

THE CHALLENGE

Effective communication is the cornerstone of a healthy relationship. Research shows that how a couple communicates is more important to the quality of the relationship than a couple's level of commitment, their personality traits, or the impact of stressful life events in predicting whether marriage will last or end in divorce.

So why is maintaining open, honest, reciprocal communication a challenge for so many couples? We fall into routines, take each other for granted, and forget to check in; we may also be limited by fears that we won't be accepted or, worse, that we will be criticized or humiliated. We may lack assertiveness or active listening skills, have different communication styles, or have our own insecurities, histories, or stories that lead us to misinterpret our partners' words or motives.

Archana and Janaka, a couple I once worked with, both grew up in families that valued avoiding conflict to "keep the peace." They developed a dynamic in which Archana would make a request indirectly while Janaka was engaged in another task, and Janaka would ignore the question. Archana would seethe and snap at Janaka for not doing what she'd asked. Janaka would withdraw for days, feeling hurt. Archana's frustration would increase until she snapped again.

This pattern is an example of what many couples experience. Through trying to avoid conflict, we develop an unhealthy pattern of relating to one another that actually generates conflict.

THE REMEDY

Effective communication is about more than just small talk. It is about expressing ourselves deeply and authentically. This requires self-awareness and a deeper understanding of our partners' personalities and communication styles. When we find ourselves misunderstanding each other, this is an opportunity to ask, "How can I better understand you and better communicate with you? What tools can help me?"

In this part, we will discuss how the Nonviolent Communication (NVC) model, developed by psychologist Marshall Rosenberg, can be used to facilitate nonjudgmental expression and empathic listening during times of conflict. NVC helps translate insights gained from mindfulness practice into language that facilitates reconciliation, increases intimacy and empathy, and fosters personal responsibility for our behaviors, actions, and thoughts. Through a simple formula that teaches us to express observations, feelings, needs, and requests, NVC can defuse heated conversations, bridge differing opinions, and shift longstanding patterns of unhealthy communication. NVC allows us to express our perspectives, feelings, and needs in a way that minimizes defensiveness and increases the likelihood our partners will hear us.

As Archana and Janaka began communicating assertively through NVC, their cycle of avoidance, passive-aggressiveness, resentment, and withdrawal unraveled. Both partners practiced using "I feel" and "I need" statements to express themselves and learned to listen to each other's requests. When the couple found themselves back in their cycle, they could identify the issue, pause, and practice their new skills.

In the following chapters, you will learn how to incorporate this communication practice into your relationship using the four components of NVC: observations, feelings, needs, and requests.

The ability to observe without evaluating is
the highest form of intelligence.

—JIDDU KRISHNAMURTI

FOUR

Observations

OBSERVATIONS VERSUS EVALUATIONS

This chapter focuses on distinguishing observations from evaluations. An *observation* is an unbiased, nonjudgmental witnessing of the facts as we perceive them with our senses. An *evaluation*, on the other hand, is the judgment, meaning, or story we have about the facts; it's how we *interpret* what we observe.

When we share an observation free from judgment or evaluation, it tends to generate feelings of respect and non-defensiveness in the listener. Conversely, when we share an observation laden with evaluation, it tends to be perceived as criticism or an attack and provokes defensive responses from the listener.

Imagine you are in the middle of a busy workweek, and you come home exhausted. As you're working on your computer, your partner puts their hand on your shoulder and says, "You clearly care more about your work than you do about this relationship." Notice how you feel in your body. Do you tense up? Collapse? Do you feel anger or fear? Do you have the urge to lash out or pull away? Do you develop a story about your partner that they are needy or aggressive or don't understand you?

Shake off those sensations, and imagine that you are in the middle of that same busy workweek. Your partner puts their hand on your shoulder and says, "I notice you've been working from seven to nine with no breaks the past three days." Imagine hearing that statement and notice how you feel in your body. What does it feel like to be observed nonjudgmentally? What stories, if any, come to mind about your partner now?

In the first example, your partner initiates the conversation with an evaluation of your behavior and imbues your behavior with a meaning that isn't necessarily true. This may cause you to feel constricted and defensive. In the second example, your partner leads with a nonjudgmental observation, which validates your experience and joins you both in a shared perspective. The statement opens up space for a discussion about how each of you is feeling about the situation.

GO DEEPER
Evaluations Versus Observations

At first it might be hard to differentiate observations from evaluations. To practice this skill, grab your journal for this solo exercise. Take as much time as needed.

1. Write out three short judgments or stories you have about your partner—these could be things that irk you or that you fight about regularly (e.g., "He never makes plans for our vacations like I ask").

2. Read these statements as though someone were making these judgments about you. As you read, notice the feelings, emotions, temperature changes in your body, sensations, urges, and thoughts that arise.

3. In a different pen color, rewrite each evaluation as an objective observation (e.g., "I asked him to make plans for an upcoming trip; the plans have not been made yet").

4. Read these objective observations as though someone said them to you, noticing how you feel in your body. Notice feelings, emotions, temperature changes in your body, sensations, urges, and thoughts.

5. Record any insights about the difference between evaluations and observations.

This week, notice when you are evaluating versus observing yourself and others. Practice restating evaluations as observations, and notice what happens. Track breakthroughs in your journal, and celebrate them with your partner!

OBSERVING YOURSELF

In the presence of another, there is more potential to feel discomfort, insecurity, and self-criticism, making it easier for us to slip into self-protective evaluations despite our best intentions. We judge and evaluate ourselves, in part, in an attempt to protect ourselves from being vulnerable, motivate ourselves to greater achievement, or communicate unmet needs. We've mistakenly learned that being critical toward ourselves is a way to take control, improve, and grow. However, self-judgment can actually undermine self-worth and intimacy with our partners.

My client Dana had a self-judgment that she could never do anything right. When Dana's wife, Anita, asked for Dana's help with the kids, Dana shut down and withdrew. She descended into a spiral of self-criticism about how she could never do anything right, which strained the relationship and left Anita feeling isolated and stressed. In therapy, Dana worked on nonjudgmentally observing the situation and her thoughts, body sensations, and emotions using a mindfulness tool called RAIN so that she could be present and available to support her partner and family. You'll learn how to do this in the following exercise.

Practice: RAIN

This solo exercise, which is a four-step process, takes about 20 minutes—5 minutes for each step in RAIN. You can practice this technique on a regular basis and during times of distress. One partner can read to the other, if you choose.

1. Set a timer for 20 minutes and sit comfortably. Close your eyes.

2. **Recognize:** Nonjudgmentally recognize and name emotions you feel in the present moment.

3. **Allow:** Acknowledge, accept, and allow your emotions to be as they are without trying to change them. Allowing does not mean you *like* what is happening, but that you allow it, dislike and all.

4. **Investigate with kindness:** Ask yourself, "What am I experiencing inside my body? What is calling my attention? What does this feeling need from me?"

5. **Non-identification/nurture with self-compassion:** Observe thoughts, feelings, and sensations without attaching to them. If you notice painful feelings, nurture them by placing a hand over your heart or speaking words of kindness, reassurance, and compassion, such as "I see you're suffering," or "I'm sorry," or "I love you, I'm listening."

6. When the timer rings, sit quietly until you are ready to open your eyes.

Notice the open-hearted awareness that emerges when you've spent time observing and nurturing yourself. Imagine how it would feel to bring this feeling into your relationship. In your journal, jot down how and when you might use this technique this week.

Like Dana, many of us have inner voices that judge us harshly and prevent us from showing up for our partners. The exercises that follow will help you apply the nonjudgmental and compassionate observation from RAIN to places where you feel most self-critical so that you can show up for your relationship from a place of presence.

Practice: RAINING ON YOUR INNER CRITIC'S PARADE

This solo exercise takes about 30 minutes and requires your journal. Review the steps of RAIN on page 58. You'll have a chance to do this with your partner later.

1. Sit comfortably. Think of an area in your life that causes you to feel self-critical and judgmental—a fear, behavior, or insecurity that strains your relationship (e.g., overworking to avoid emotions or conflict, insecurity about your appearance, or a behavior you feel shame about).

2. In your journal, create three columns with the headers "Thoughts and Judgments," "Feelings," and "Nurturing Alternative."

3. **Recognize:** Set a timer for 5 minutes. Call to mind your focus. Recognize thoughts and judgments that arise. What words, phrases, or tone do you use toward yourself? What does this critical, judgmental voice feel like? When the timer rings, jot down the thoughts and judgments you noticed in your journal under "Thoughts and Judgments."

4. **Allow and Investigate:** Reset the timer for 10 minutes. Call your focus to mind. Notice and allow the physical sensations and emotions you feel to be as they are. Ask yourself, "What is calling my attention? What does this feeling need or want for me?" When the timer rings, jot down under the "Feelings" column any feelings that arose for you.

5. **Non-identification/nurture:** Reset the timer for 5 minutes. As you recall your focus, bring nurturing to these feelings through soothing self-talk and a gentle tone, the way you would talk to a loved one. Notice if the situation unfolds differently in your mind's eye as you bring nonjudgment and compassion to it. When the timer rings, jot down under the "Nurturing Alternative" column how you can nurture yourself when you feel self-critical this week and how this approach could affect your partner and your relationship.

The tone we use with ourselves often can influence how we speak with our partners. By observing ourselves more clearly and compassionately, we are able to be more present and available, and see our partners with fewer projections or judgments.

OBSERVING YOUR PARTNER

Just as self-judgment prevents us from responding flexibly to the present moment, judging our partners constrains them and limits our ability to receive and appreciate them as they are. If we can transform our evaluations into compassionate observation, we create space for deeper empathy, intimacy, and connection.

Take for instance a session I had with Ling and Trent: Ling was explaining her belief that Trent was inauthentic around their friends. Ling said her intention was to support Trent in "being his best self." Trent expressed that he didn't feel understood and felt like he'd rather spend time with friends without Ling around so he didn't have to "walk on eggshells."

We focused on uncoupling Ling's evaluation from her observation of Trent. As Ling nonjudgmentally shared her observations of Trent's behaviors, Trent listened, explained why he acted differently in different contexts, and expressed his experience that Ling was judging a core part of his identity. Ling noted she felt more understanding and accepting of Trent, which helped her feel closer to him. She shared that she could let go of her judgments about Trent's actions and see the situation from another point of view.

As with Ling and Trent, our attempt to help our partners grow by offering evaluations can backfire, leading our partners to feel misunderstood, to pull away, and to reject our feedback. If we can step back in these moments and instead observe our partners as they are, we can see our partners in a new way and create space for them to grow. The following exercise helps create a nonjudgmental space to notice and discuss your different experiences so that you can feel more understood even when your perspectives differ.

Practice: HEART TALKS

This joint exercise should take about 20 minutes and requires your journals. You'll need a "talking stick" for this exercise. It doesn't have to be an actual stick; I recommend a heart-shaped stone. The person holding the object will be the speaker and the other will be the listener until the object is passed.

1. Together, choose a mildly bothersome relationship issue. The point is not to try to resolve this issue, but to practice having difficult conversations in a nonjudgmental way.

2. In your journals, spend several minutes writing about the chosen issue using observations rather than evaluations.

3. Sit comfortably facing each other, and set a timer for 15 minutes.

4. Make eye contact. Whoever wants to speak first can pick up the object.

5. The speaker will describe the issue in their own words using observations. If a sense of charge arises, notice this—often feeling a charge can propel us into evaluation. The goal is not to attach judgment to your partner's actions.

6. The listener's job is to just listen and observe. If the listener has an urge to interrupt, their job is to just notice the accompanying feelings and sensations in themselves.

7. When the speaker is finished, the object is passed to the listener and they may now share their observation of the situation.

8. Take turns passing the object and sharing observations.

9. If the conversation becomes heated, pause, take a deep breath together, and restart where you left off.

10. When the timer rings, respond to the following questions in your journals:

    ◈ How did you feel observing your partner?
    ◈ Being observed?
    ◈ Sharing observations?

Discuss this activity and your reflections with your partner.

Despite our best intentions, we will sometimes get angry and take our anger out on our partners by evaluating or judging their actions rather than observing them—and vice versa. In these moments, forgiveness is an important practice. Extending forgiveness doesn't mean condoning one's behavior, but rather letting go of judgments that create more pain and suffering, and instead practicing observation and acceptance. When we forgive, we become more open, compassionate, generous, and able to see our partners with fresh eyes.

This practice is adapted from an exercise in *The Mindful Self-Compassion Workbook* by Kristin Neff, PhD, and Christopher Germer, PhD. It is designed to help you forgive your partner for an action that led you to feel pain or suffering. If you don't feel especially angry, you can practice alongside your partner; otherwise, do it solo. This exercise should take about 20 minutes and calls for your journal.

1. Sit comfortably, and call to mind a mildly distressing situation you feel ready to forgive.

2. In your journal, jot down your recollection of the situation based on *observations* of the behaviors, events, thoughts, and feelings that occurred.

3. Set a timer for 10 minutes, and close your eyes.

4. **Open:** Feel and allow the pain in your body.

5. **Self-compassion:** Validate the pain with compassionate words and a soothing touch, perhaps noting, "Of course you feel hurt," or putting a hand over your heart. Stay on this step as long as you feel the need to.

6. **Wisdom and empathy:** Acknowledge that your partner made a mistake and was influenced by circumstances you might not understand. Remember times that you made mistakes and wished for forgiveness.

7. **Forgiveness breath:** Cultivate a feeling of forgiveness in your heart that you will send to your partner. With each inhale, expand this feeling of forgiveness, and with each exhale, extend forgiveness and compassion toward the situation and your partner. You can use phrases like "May I begin to forgive you. . ." or repeat "Forgive" at the top of each breath as a mantra.

8. When the timer rings, take a moment to notice how you feel in your body. If done with your partner, open your eyes and make compassionate eye contact while continuing the forgiveness breath for several more breaths.

If you felt like you were struggling to find forgiveness, repeat this practice daily, adapting it as needed. You can go deeper with the practice by writing a letter (which you can choose to send or not) that includes observations of the situation from your perspective, what you appreciated about the person, what you learned, and your willingness to make amends.

Time spent observing yourself and your partner in meditation and everyday life are important for developing more clarity when emotions and thoughts arise in moments of conflict. These skills provide an important foundation for being able to observe your relationship from a bird's-eye view.

OBSERVING YOUR RELATIONSHIP

We develop cycles in our relationships based on each partner's innate tendencies that may be functional in some situations but limiting in others. For example, one partner may be more emotionally expressive and do all the organizational tasks for the couple whereas the other is focused on their job or schooling, but when circumstances change—perhaps the couple moves or the family is struck by hardship—this particular way of relating to each other may no longer meet the couple's emotional needs.

The first step to shifting a cycle is to observe the cycle and how our perceptions and attributions drive the behaviors that contribute to it. When we recognize a cycle is at play—that our fight is generated by a dynamic and not the content about which we are arguing—we can begin to defuse our reactions and alter our behaviors and our cycle.

Chris and Arun are a young couple that came to therapy for grief support while Chris's brother battled a critical illness. Chris's grief led him to pull away from Arun, which activated Arun's feelings of abandonment. Chris felt guilty and self-critical about how his behavior impacted Arun, causing him to pull away even more. This dynamic undermined the closeness the couple desperately wanted. In therapy, each partner started to observe how their actions contributed to the reactive cycle between them. Arun noted that his tendency to demand that Chris share his feelings came from Arun's fear of abandonment but caused Chris to feel pressure and pull away. Chris noted his tendency to pull away was an effort to avoid feelings of shame, loss, and disconnection but actually left him feeling more disconnected.

Through mindful observation of the cycle and identification of underlying feelings and needs using the RAIN tool, the couple learned to understand and respond to their partner's feelings rather than to their reactive behaviors. Each partner was able to make small changes to their behavior that altered the cycle as whole.

Practice: RAINING ON RELATIONSHIP DYNAMICS

This joint exercise takes about 30 minutes and calls for your journals. This is the same exercise as "RAINing on Your Inner Critic's Parade" with the exception of the first and last steps.

1. Sit comfortably beside each other. Together, choose a recent fight that represents a familiar dynamic in your relationship.

2. Follow steps 2 through 5 on page 59 in the exercise "RAINing on Your Inner Critic's Parade."

3. When the last timer rings, share your experience with your partner. Using observational statements, discuss ways you contribute to the dynamic you chose in step 1.

Each partner can commit to one thing they will practice doing differently this week, whether this is changing evaluations to observations, practicing seeing things from the other's perspective, or altering a specific behavior. After sharing this commitment with your partner, make a note of what you will commit to in your journal and highlight it.

Another way to understand and become less vulnerable to our triggers is to identify them using the psychology technique, behavioral chain analysis (BCA). This technique is based on the idea that our problem behaviors arise for a reason; each problem behavior is actually an adaptive way to meet a need. Even behaviors that cause problems—like withdrawing or yelling at our partners when we're upset—also serve a function or give us something we want.

BCA helps you visualize the chain of events leading up to the problem behavior; understand emotions, thoughts, behaviors, and contexts that trigger it; and reflect on how to respond differently in the future. Here are the basic links on the chain:

◈ Problem behavior: The behavior you're trying to change.

◈ Vulnerability: A stressor that heightens your susceptibility to being triggered (e.g., stress, hunger, lack of sleep, pain, drinking, a fight, a recent loss, etc.).

◈ Prompting event: The event that led to your problem behavior (e.g., your partner yelled at you).

◈ Links: Thoughts and feelings that happen as a result of the prompting event and the actions you took right after the prompting event. Consider in detail what happened right after the prompting event took place. What happened after that? And then what happened after that? And so on.

◈ Consequences: How your problem behavior affects you and others.

Practice: BEHAVIORAL CHAIN ANALYSIS

This solo exercise takes about 10 minutes and calls for your journal. You can draw a visual BCA by following the diagram and steps outlined here.

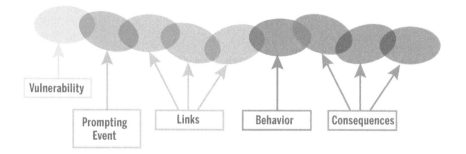

1. In your journal, identify the **problem behavior** you want to change (e.g., snapping at your partner).

2. To identify your **vulnerability**, think back to what was happening before the difficult situation arose.

3. Identify **links**: Note each thought, feeling, and body sensation you experienced in response to these circumstances as links on the chain (e.g., "I should be able to handle this," "overwhelmed," or "increased heart rate").

4. List behaviors that your thoughts, feelings, and sensations led to (e.g., actions to escape the situation, snapping, or addictive behaviors).

5. Note the positive and negative **consequences** that occurred from the problem behavior. How did you feel afterward? Better? Disappointed? Ashamed?

Notice the next time you are in a similar situation. Are you more aware of your triggers? Is the frequency, duration, or intensity of the problem behavior less than before? Make a note of this in your journal. Do this exercise as soon as possible after a problematic reaction to decrease feelings of guilt, fear, and shame and to help you respond more mindfully next time.

When you can identify feelings, thoughts, and behaviors that lead you to react in habitual ways in your relationship, you gain insight and information that allow you to try on new ways of responding to your trigger.

Wrap-Up

◈ Evaluations tend to evoke defensive responses, whereas observations tend to invite discussion.

◈ Through the practice of RAIN (recognizing, allowing, investigating, and non-identification/nurturing), we can transform our relationship to ourselves, our partners, and the relationship itself.

◈ Nonjudgmental witnessing of the facts can change the dynamic of a conversation.

◈ Forgiveness is possible when we let go of judgments and practice observation and acceptance of our partners.

If you do not know what you feel,
then it is difficult to choose love.

—BELL HOOKS

ALL ABOUT LOVE: NEW VISIONS

FIVE

Feelings

THINKING VERSUS FEELING

Perhaps you've noticed that although feelings may arise in reaction to thoughts, there is no formula for how our thoughts will impact our emotions. One day, the thought "I should comfort my partner" may evoke compassion, and another day, the same thought may evoke anger or annoyance. Because there is no formula, it is important to practice discerning thoughts from feelings so we can respond to each thought or feeling as it arises in the moment.

Thoughts and feelings that seem to arise simultaneously may feel overwhelming and provoke us to react. By slowing down and recognizing the chain of thoughts and feelings occurring inside of us, we can instead respond in a way that's aligned with our values. When I work with my clients, we practice observing thoughts, identifying feelings, and noticing the overarching pattern in which this cascade of thoughts and feelings arises. Once we identify these, clients begin to experience greater emotional freedom. Studies show that being able to unlink our feelings from the ruminative thoughts we have about them is the key to helping difficult emotions pass.

In a session with Rose and Malik, Malik expressed that he believed the relationship would be healthier if the couple were having more sex. Rose responded that she thought Malik was wrong and was hurt by his insensitivity to her chronic pain. When Rose and Malik slowed down this interaction and practiced observing their thoughts and feelings, Malik was able to express that his feeling was a desire to be closer to Rose and his thought was that she didn't find him attractive. Rose noticed that her initial feeling response to Malik's statement was surprise and fear, and her thought was that Malik did not understand her and might break up with her. When Malik shared his thoughts and feelings, Rose noted that she felt more receptive to Malik when he spoke this way. Malik noted that he felt closer to Rose as well.

Like Malik and Rose, we all experience times where our partners' expression of a thought or feeling about a sensitive subject evokes uncomfortable feelings or a defensive reaction before we even really understand what they are trying to communicate. By discerning our own thoughts and feelings, we can communicate them to our partners in a way that brings us closer. The following meditation will help you practice noticing thoughts and feelings.

Practice: NOTICING THOUGHTS AND FEELINGS

This 10-minute meditation can be done solo or alongside your partner.

1. Sit comfortably, and set a timer for 10 minutes. Close your eyes.

2. As your focus, choose a situation between you and your partner that leads you to feel defensive or uncomfortable.

3. Breathe normally, following your breath in and out.

4. Imagine your awareness as a clear, blue sky, and visualize each thought, feeling, or sensation that arises as a cloud passing through the sky. Some thoughts may be dark and heavy and linger or create storms; others may be lighter and pass quickly.

5. If you become distracted, simply return to observing these clouds.

6. Unpleasant thoughts may accompany uncomfortable feelings. Instead of trying to change or resist thoughts or feelings, simply allow, accept, and watch these clouds pass by or shift.

7. When the timer rings, return your attention to your breath and open your eyes. Recall your focus and notice how you feel about it now.

When we identify and practice detaching from challenging thoughts and feelings, we can more easily allow our emotions to flow without changing, suppressing, or controlling them. When we feel overwhelmed, we often distract ourselves to avoid the feeling, but research tells us that turning toward our feelings instead actually allows them to dissipate more quickly.

Expansion is a practice used in Acceptance and Commitment Therapy (ACT) that involves accepting and allowing difficult, overwhelming, and unpleasant feelings and sensations to expand and flow through us without resistance. Unlike the previous meditation, which includes thoughts and sensations, expansion focuses on making contact with the feelings as they arise in our bodies.

Practice: EXPANSION

This 10-minute meditation can be done solo or alongside your partner.

1. Sit comfortably, and set a timer for 10 minutes. Close your eyes. Breathe normally, following your breath in and out.

2. Focus on a situation between you and your partner that evokes feelings of discomfort or simply focus on whatever emotions are present in the moment.

3. Bring your awareness to your emotions. If you become distracted by thoughts, gently return awareness to your emotions as you take the following steps:

   ◈ Observe: Notice, observe, and allow your emotions to flow. If you notice several emotions, rest your attention on one for now.
   ◈ Breathe: Breathe in and allow this emotion to expand. Move closer to it rather than avoiding it.
   ◈ Create space: Give yourself permission to feel this emotion without evaluating whether you like or dislike it.
   ◈ Allow: Continue allowing the emotion to flow through you as would energy, a cloud, smoke, or water.

4. When the timer rings, return your attention to your breath for several inhalations and open your eyes. Take a moment to notice how you feel in your body.

Distinguishing thoughts from feelings and truly allowing our feelings help us to better manage our emotions so we can show up in our relationship with more responsiveness to our partners and less reactivity. Aim to practice this meditation daily.

TUNING IN TO HOW YOU FEEL

The relationship we have with others begins with the relationship we have with ourselves. When we lovingly notice, identify, and accept our own emotions and deep needs, we can show up lovingly for our partners to do the same.

Ideally, when we're developing as children and express an emotion, our caregivers reflect that emotion back to us through attuned words, gestures, and actions. In this way, we learn to identify our feelings and respond to them. For some of us, this process is disrupted if we're taught to suppress or ignore our emotions (e.g., we feel sad and a parent doesn't notice, focuses on their own sadness, or communicates "You have nothing to be sad about; focus on the positive"). We are taught to "buck up," "tough it out," or "deal with it," or we are bullied for being "weak" or "a wimp." We learn to ignore our emotions and internalize the notion that expressing them creates conflict or inconvenience for others.

In truth, all emotions have a purpose, and expressing our emotions allows us to define ourselves, feel more satisfied, and connect more deeply with our partner. For example, sadness might remind us of our need to slow down and focus on healing, reflection, or a transition to new circumstances. Expressing our sadness may let our partners know that we are struggling and have needs. If we suppress this sadness rather than acknowledge it, it can become depression or lead us to unhealthy coping skills such as self-medicating through alcohol, shopping, or food, which can negatively impact our relationships.

When people enter therapy for the first time, they are often unaware of what they are feeling and may even feel shame when they start identifying feelings. Through mindfulness and tools such as those described in the following exercises, clients start gaining self-awareness and communicating to their partners with more ease. One body-based mindfulness tool that involves listening to physiological sensations is adapted from a technique called Focusing. I use it with clients to help them access, attune to, and articulate emotions that might be hard to define.

Practice: FOCUSING

This joint exercise should take about 10 to 20 minutes per partner. You will trade off guiding each other. The speaker will slowly read the dialogue, waiting as long as necessary for the receiver to speak the answer aloud between prompts.

1. Sit or lie comfortably, and close your eyes.

2. **Listen:** Pay attention inwardly to your body. What physical sensations are calling your attention? Where are these located in your body? (For example, perhaps you feel anxious tightening in your throat, heaviness in your chest, or a knot in your stomach.)

3. **Get a sense of feeling:** As your focus area, choose whatever concern or sensation feels strongest. Feel the unclear sense of this feeling.

4. **Describe:** Where exactly is the feeling—deep in your body or on the surface? What color is this feeling? What shape? What size? What texture? Is it hard and smooth or rough and jagged? Is it moving or still? Observe the qualities of this feeling.

5. **Name:** Allow an image, word, or phrase to arise from these sensations. It may be a feeling word like "scared" or "anxious"; a quality word like "tight," "sticky," or "scary"; or simply an image. If the word feels intellectual, discard it, and wait for a feeling word that resonates. This may take a few minutes. If nothing arises, simply feel the quality and move to the next step.

6. **Resonate:** Feel if the word, phrase, or image resonates; there may be a release or softening, or the feeling's intensity may decrease. Allow the word, phrase, or image to change to fit the feeling.

7. **Ask and receive:** What does this place need? Listen for the answer from within.

Whether you experienced a shift, you have practiced spending time sensing and feeling your body, which helps create more awareness and ability to express your emotions.

Sitting with painful feelings is difficult. The next practice is adapted from an exercise in *The Mindful Self-Compassion Workbook* by Kristin Neff, PhD, and Christopher Germer, PhD. It helps you "soften" into uncomfortable feelings with compassion, allowing you to open to greater intimacy with your partners. By being with the pain and sitting together in difficult moments, you can avoid reacting to them, through lashing out, pursuing, or avoiding.

Practice: SOFTEN, SOOTHE, ALLOW

This joint practice takes about 15 minutes. It can be used regularly or during difficult times in your relationship.

1. Sit comfortably side by side, perhaps with a hand touching each other. Set a timer for 10 minutes, and close your eyes.

2. Call to mind a difficult situation if one is not immediately present.

3. Place a hand over your heart or whichever body part you feel the painful or difficult emotions.

4. Silently label in a gentle compassionate voice any emotions you identify (e.g., sadness, grief, fear, longing, despair, etc.).

5. **Soften** into the difficult feelings in your body, as if relaxing in warm water. Hold the feelings tenderly without trying to change them.

6. **Soothe** yourself by placing your hand on your heart or where the pain is and breathe into this place. Feel the support and warmth of your hand. In your mind, speak kindly to this place as you would a child or friend (e.g., "It's difficult to feel this," "I am sorry you feel this," or "I love you").

7. **Allow** your feelings to be as they are, letting the discomfort come and go.

8. Repeat the soften-soothe-allow cycle, perhaps using the phrase repeatedly as a reminder: "Soften, soothe, allow. Soften, soothe, allow."

9. When the timer rings, open your eyes and make eye contact with your partner.

10. Spend time sitting together, without needing to speak, feeling your feelings and allowing conversation to arise (or not) naturally.

Learning to observe and be with our emotions is a skill. The more time we spend in mindful inquiry noticing, labeling, and expressing our feelings, the more adept we become at understanding, tending to, and expressing them. It can be helpful to take time to integrate and bring these feelings into expression through writing, as with the following "Go Deeper" exercise.

GO DEEPER
Naming Your Emotions

This practice is adapted from an exercise that my colleague Shrein Bahrami, licensed marriage and family therapist (LMFT), shared with me. You will need your journal. You can do this solo or alongside your partner.

1. In your journal, make a list of at least 15 emotions. If you have difficulty, do an internet search using the phrase "feelings wheel" or "feeling charts." You can also visit The Center for Nonviolent Communication (CNVC) website for a "Feelings Inventory" (see the resources at the end of this book on page 151). These resources ("feelings wheel" and "feelings") are also available on my website, LaurenKorshakMFT.com/client-portal.

2. Categorize these emotions into three groups: 1) "My most common feelings in my relationship," 2) "My most uncomfortable feelings in my relationship," and 3) "Feelings I most resist and avoid in my relationship."

3. In your journal, reflect without judgment on thoughts that arise from categorizing these feelings. Note what life experiences may have contributed to the emotions you chose and what might be preventing you from facing some of the more difficult feelings now.

If you did this exercise together, spend a few minutes discussing your insights.

TUNING IN TO YOUR
PARTNER'S FEELINGS

Often we can become so identified with our own feelings and perspectives that we don't receive our partners as they are, leading us to feel disconnected and isolated during times we need each other most.

If instead, like Rose and Malik, we can step outside of our defensive reactions and compassionately receive our partners, our partners feel seen, and we develop a greater sense of connection in our relationship. "Eyes On" is a practice intended to help you be with your own feelings and projections as you compassionately witness your partner.

Practice: EYES ON

This joint practice should take 10 or more minutes. It is best to record the instructions (read slowly), and then listen together. I've included a recording of the instructions on my website under LaurenKorshakMFT.com/meditations.html. Alternatively, one partner can do the "Breath Awareness" practice on page 6, while the other does this exercise.

1. Sit facing your partner.

2. Close your eyes and notice thoughts, sensations, and emotions in your body.

3. Softly open your eyes. Take in your partner across from you. See that your partner also experiences emotions, sensations, thoughts, and breath. Sometimes your partner feels happy or loved or proud.

4. Close your eyes again and notice the thoughts, emotions, and sensations present inside of you as you did before. Notice and welcome any difficult emotions you are feeling.

5. Softly open your eyes again and take in your partner across from you. See that your partner also sometimes hurts, feels pain, sadness, fear, and suffering.

6. Close your eyes and notice what you are feeling. Breathe into it. Notice areas of tension or fear, warmth or empathy, compassion or love.

7. Cultivate a feeling of appreciation in your heart for your partner and their willingness to see you and be seen.

Afterward, discuss your experience and whether this is a practice you would like to repeat. This practice deepens through consistent use.

—◆—

Intimately tuning in to your partner's feelings necessitates that you honestly assert and actively listen to each other's perspective. Assertiveness is the capacity to ask for what you want and is best done using "I" statements. Active listening is the ability to communicate your understanding to your partner by restating their message and entails listening deeply to the content, feelings, and tone of the speaker without interruption.

Practice: PERSPECTIVE-TAKING THROUGH ASSERTIVENESS AND ACTIVE LISTENING

This joint exercise, which should take 10 to 25 minutes, helps you practice assertiveness and active listening with your partner while discussing an issue you disagree on. The point is not to solve the issue or come to an agreement, but to practice these skills, better understand your partner's feelings, and create connection across differing perspectives.

1. Pick a situation in which you and your partner have different perspectives. You will take turns sharing your perspective.

2. One partner will be the speaker and will share first, practicing the assertiveness skill of using "I" statements (e.g., "I observe . . ." and "I feel . . .") as they share their perspective.

3. The listener will practice active listening by receiving their partner's words, tone, and body language without interruption, while noticing their own bodily responses and feelings.

4. When the speaker has finished, the listener will reflect on what they have heard (e.g., "What I heard you say is . . .") and share what

they heard. If the listener is confused, they can ask for clarification but should not argue with the speaker's perspective.

5. If the speaker does not feel heard, they can continue rephrasing their perspective until the listener is able to accurately reflect it back.

6. Once the speaker feels the listener has heard them, switch roles.

It can be hard to feel connected as a couple when difficult feelings or differing opinions surface, but if you can turn toward your feelings and each other with compassion and willingness to vulnerably express yourselves and humbly listen, doors will open in your relationship you never knew existed.

Wrap-Up

◈ All emotions have a purpose, and mindfully expressing our emotions allows us to connect more deeply with our partners.

◈ Mindfulness practices and journaling are useful ways to tune in to our feelings.

◈ When we allow rather than resist difficult feelings, we create deeper intimacy with ourselves and our partner.

◈ Compassionately witnessing our emotions together creates connection in difficult moments that might otherwise divide us.

◈ Active listening and assertiveness are learnable skills that help us understand our partners and foster more connected conversations.

As long as you hold onto wanting something
from the outside, you will be dissatisfied
because there is a part of you that you are
still not totally owning . . . How can you be
complete and fulfilled if you believe that
you cannot own this part [of yourself] until
somebody else does something?

—A. H. ALMAAS

SIX

Needs and Requests

NEEDS VERSUS PREFERENCES

Distinguishing needs from preferences is important. Preferences are a desire for one alternative over another and are often a way in which we attempt to meet our needs. Needs are essential driving forces required for health and well-being that, when ignored or denied, lead to adverse outcomes that interfere with our well-being and relationships.

You would think it would be easy to distinguish needs from preferences, but needs can be tricky to identify. We may minimize a need by assuming it's a preference, only to notice ourselves lashing out later. Alternatively, we may become attached to a preference as the *only* way to satisfy a need that we haven't yet identified. Imagine you were out hiking in the middle of nowhere with only a water bottle but you were craving soda, and you became upset that you couldn't have soda. Your need would be thirst, which could be satisfied by many different beverages, and your preference would be soda.

By recognizing our needs, we can be more flexible with our partners than if we remain attached to preferences. For example, let's say you have a preference for only attending events if your partner attends with you. The underlying need may be to feel security, but the preference that your partner attend every event is a strategy to meet that need. Your preference may not always be feasible and could cause your partner to feel stifled. By identifying your underlying need for security, you can explore other strategies to meet this need—perhaps through mindfulness or self-soothing tools, or checking in with your partner by text or phone during the event.

This solo practice requires only a few minutes and your journal.

1. Sit comfortably in a quiet place.

2. In your journal, list recent requests you've made of your partner.

3. When your list is complete, identify whether your request was made to fill a need or if it was a preference. For example, perhaps you asked your partner to run errands with you, but what you needed was to spend quality time with them.

4. When you've identified a preference, jot down ideas for reframing the request so it speaks to the underlying need you were trying to have met. For example, you could let your partner know that you need some quality time together, and running errands would be one way to fill that need.

If you find yourself disproportionately emotional or reactive in response to a situation, there is a good chance your emotion is pointing to a deeper, unmet need. For example, you might notice yourself feeling angry when your need for freedom is not met or happy when your need for appreciation is satisfied.

Painful feelings like anger, despair, or envy often reveal an unmet need, whereas feelings of ease and well-being usually indicate that our needs are mostly being met. To help discover your needs, the Center for Nonviolent Communication includes a "needs inventory" and a "feelings inventory" on their website (see resources at the end of this book on page 151). You can also find them ("My Needs" and "Feelings") under the "Client Portal" on my website, LaurenKorshakMFT.com. Download these inventories, which we will be using in the following exercise, to start exploring your needs.

GO DEEPER

Feelings and Needs List

This solo exercise highlights the connection between needs and feelings. It should take about 20 minutes and calls for your journal.

1. Review the CNVC needs and feelings inventories from their website.

2. Recall a situation with your partner in which you felt unsatisfied, angry, or another feeling on the "unsatisfied" feelings list. Notice which emotions and physical sensations arise as you recall this situation, and note these in your journal.

3. Review the needs inventory, and list all your unmet needs in that situation.

4. For each unmet need, jot down one or two ways the need could have been met or could be met next time the situation arises. For example, if your need was for connection, you could touch your partner or ask for a hug, or if the need was for autonomy, you could ask for alone time.

YOUR NEEDS

Have you ever dismissed a desire to ask your partner to stop what they are doing so that you could eat dinner together, only to find yourself hangry and accuse them hours later of being selfish? Or have you ever had a melt-down over your partner leaving a dish in the sink and found yourself feeling increasingly bereft and angry? In many daily instances, our underlying needs get ignored for a variety of reasons, leading us to react in ways that seem disproportionate to a given situation. We may ignore our needs because we were taught that having needs means we are needy, indulgent, or selfish. Or we may fear that stating our needs will cause our partners to leave or not like us.

We all have needs that must be met for us to thrive, and understanding these needs is essential to a healthy partnership. Denying our needs leads to resentment and an inability to soothe ourselves in our relationships. Accepting our needs allows us to self-soothe, understand our partners, and better navigate the ups and downs of our relationships. Needs include physical necessities, like the need for sleep or food, and emotional necessities, like the need for connection, meaning, honesty, play, peace, and autonomy.

By now you may be starting to recognize that getting your needs met doesn't just magically happen; it's crucial to acknowledge that it is our job to recognize and meet our own needs. Our partners can support us and be there to listen and help, but identifying and expressing our needs is ultimately our responsibility.

Taking time to reflect on your needs deepens your self-awareness, leads to feelings of well-being, and lays the foundation for you to be a present, available, understanding, and humble partner. The following exercise can help you start developing a deeper relationship with your needs.

Practice: IDENTIFYING MY NEEDS

Grab your journal for this solo exercise and sit in a quiet place. Spend about 15 minutes responding to the prompts.

1. In your journal, list your needs in this moment, referencing the needs inventory you downloaded earlier or the "My Needs" handout under the "Client Portal" on my website, LaurenKorshakMFT.com.

2. Review the needs on your list. If there is something you can ask for, circle it. If there is something you can do for yourself, underline it.

3. In your journal, reflect on the following:

   ◈ What are some ways you "drop hints" about your needs without asking for them directly?

   ◈ Describe a time you used behavior instead of words to get your needs met.

   ◈ How is your relationship affected by the way you get your needs met? Is there room to meet your needs differently or more directly (e.g., expressing them out loud or asking for help)?

Put your insights from this exercise into action. Schedule time to check in with yourself by pausing and asking yourself what you need. Keep a screenshot of the needs inventory on your phone for support identifying your needs during these check-ins.

The needs inventory along with the following "Identifying Deeper Patterns" exercise helped Kevin and Roya, a couple I worked with, stay together and develop a solid foundation for their relationship.

Kevin and Roya came to therapy to save their budding relationship. After several months of dating, Roya expressed anger for the first time and Kevin withdrew. Two days later, Kevin unexpectedly told Roya he wanted to end the relationship. He stated that his needs weren't being met, but he couldn't articulate what those needs were. After working with the needs inventory in therapy, Kevin identified unmet needs for acceptance, quality time, and being heard. By identifying and expressing these needs, Kevin was able to feel heard, and the couple discussed ways to address these needs together, such as through scheduling quality time and heart talks. For Kevin, learning to state his needs led to feelings of empowerment and, ultimately, to relief that he didn't have to reactively leave the relationship against his deeper wishes.

Like Kevin, many of us have felt overwhelmed by feelings we don't understand and end up reacting in ways that conflict with our deeper wishes. Learning to identify underlying needs offers us freedom to respond to and express our needs in wholehearted ways that align with our values. The following exercise helped Kevin understand how his reactions to his needs were influenced by past experiences in addition to his temperament and helped him verbalize to Roya needs that had not been acknowledged or validated in his childhood.

Needs that were unmet in childhood with early caregivers can get displaced and projected onto our relationship. Bringing awareness to these early unmet needs can help dispel patterns of dissatisfaction and projection in your relationship.

Practice: IDENTIFYING DEEPER PATTERNS

This solo exercise is adapted from psychotherapist David Richo's work on the five aspects of love, which are also foundational relationship needs: 1) attention, 2) acceptance, 3) appreciation, 4) affection, and 5) allowing. Grab your journal and sit in a quiet place. Spend about 30 minutes responding to the prompts.

1. In your journal, make three columns and label them "Needs," "Met," and "Unmet."

2. Under "Needs," list five to seven important relationship needs using the five aspects of love as a starting point. Refer to the needs inventory you downloaded earlier, and add or swap out other needs.

3. Under "Met," note the ways these needs were met for you in your childhood (e.g., your need for affection was met through words).

4. Under "Unmet," note the ways in which these needs were not met (e.g., your need for affection was not met through touch).

5. Look over your list and do the following:

    ◈ Place a star next to patterns that show up in your relationships.
    ◈ Circle patterns that are different from your current relationship.
    ◈ Underline patterns you would like to do something about.

6. In your journal, reflect on the following:

- ⬦ How are my partnership needs influenced by my patterns?
- ⬦ Do I see any patterns indicating that I am seeking needs that were met or unmet in my childhood?

At a later time that works for both partners, discuss your insights from this exercise to help you understand each other more deeply.

Seeing the root of your own needs clearly can help you detach from your stories, and see your partner and their needs in a new light.

YOUR PARTNER'S NEEDS

Healthy relationships require a balance between tending to your own needs and supporting those of your partner. Prioritizing your partner's needs over your own can lead to codependent patterns and resentment, whereas focusing too much on your own needs and not enough on your partner's can lead to disconnection, lack of intimacy, and bitterness. When you attune to your own needs, you can be more present and available to notice and help attend to your partner's needs without projecting, resenting, or misunderstanding them.

The capacity to stay in contact with your own needs and feelings while staying in contact with your partner is an aspect of healthy differentiation. The ability to differentiate your needs from your partner's helps you manage anxiety, self-soothe, understand your partner, and become less reliant on them to meet your needs or expectations.

This is a full-body awareness tool created by David Schnarch, PhD, designed to support meeting your own needs while maintaining contact with your partner. This joint practice should take about 15 minutes.

1. Get comfortable, either sitting or lying on your backs side by side.

2. For a few minutes, progressively tense and relax each set of muscles from the top of your head down to your toes by clenching your muscles on each inhale and releasing on each exhale (e.g., scrunch your eyes on an inhale and release on an exhale). For assistance, follow along with a guided "progressive muscle relaxation" recording, which you can find on the internet.

3. When you've completed the muscle relaxation exercise, stand up and face your partner. (As a variation, you can face each other while lying down.)

4. Close your eyes. Feel your breath.

5. Open your eyes and move toward your partner until you are close enough to have one foot between your partner's feet and vice versa.

6. Put your arms around each other, maintaining your balance if standing.

7. Notice and follow your breath. With each inhale, imagine you are holding your partner in their entirety. With each exhale, let your partner hold you.

8. Stay focused on yourself: Notice and allow feelings, emotions, and sensations. Notice if you feel the urge to lean in or pull away.

9. Silently use nurturing self-talk to soothe any discomfort that arises.

10. Stay here as long as you like, noticing how your body sensations and emotions shift.

When you finish, discuss the experience. Did this level of closeness feel like not enough, too much, or just right? How does this quality of contact and level of contact differ from your usual dynamic? Note any takeaways in your journal.

Another aspect of becoming more aware of your partner's needs is to understand, rather than react to, your own and your partner's anger. As you've learned, anger is a feeling that points to an unmet need. When this need is unconscious and hasn't been identified, the resulting anger may be directed at people closest to us. Identifying and meeting the need underneath anger can help defuse patterns of conflict and hurt.

In Chris and Arun's relationship, taking care of Chris's brother during his critical illness had led both partners to neglect their needs. To address this, Arun restarted individual therapy and introduced some new self-care habits. In the short-term, this seemed to backfire: When Arun would leave for yoga or to see friends, Chris would feel angry and abandoned, and Arun would feel guilty and unsure of what to do.

As Chris and Arun practiced identifying their needs, Chris began to recognize his unmet needs for grieving, affection, connection, touch, and self-care. He realized that his feelings of depression, anger, and abandonment were caused by his neglect of his own needs and grief about losing his brother, not by Arun's actions. Arun's leaving was a trigger to Chris because it forced Chris to recognize his unspoken needs. He also recognized that his bitter behavior toward Arun undermined his needs for affection and closeness with his partner. With this new awareness, the couple practiced meeting their deeper needs together, using the next exercise.

Chris and Arun's story demonstrates how unmet needs in one partner can lead to anger, resentment, and controlling behavior toward the other partner, and how expressing and tending to unmet needs can lead to greater intimacy.

Practice: UNDERNEATH ANGER MEDITATION

This 20- to 30-minute solo meditation is adapted from an exercise in *The Mindful Self-Compassion Workbook* by Kristin Neff, PhD, and Christopher Germer, PhD. It is designed to bring awareness, validation, and compassion to the needs that often underlie anger. You can record yourself reading the script (read slowly) and play it back, or have your partner or therapist guide you. If your partner guides you, wait a day before sharing your experience so you have time to process what arises.

1. Sit comfortably, and close your eyes. Take several deep breaths.

2. Call to mind a mildly bothersome situation in which you felt anger with your partner.

3. Silently notice and name your emotions.

4. Validate your emotions using compassionate, validating words and tone (e.g., "Of course you felt angry").

5. Ask yourself what you needed in this situation that you didn't get. Was it acknowledgment? Connection? Appreciation? Respect? Something else?

6. What words did you need to hear from your partner?

7. If it feels right, place a hand over your heart or the part of your body where you feel activated. Compassionately repeat to yourself the phrases you needed to hear. Try to let them in.

8. When complete, reflect in your journal:
   ◈ How did it feel to validate the anger?
   ◈ How did it feel to acknowledge the need?
   ◈ How did it feel to say the phrases to yourself?

You can do this exercise any time you feel one of the "unsatisfied" feelings on the CNVC feelings inventory to help you identify underlying unmet needs. If you share this with your partner at a later time, your partner's instructions are to listen to your experience without interruption.

MAKING AND RECEIVING REQUESTS

Now that you've practiced observing and identifying feelings and needs, it's time to practice making and receiving requests. It's important to distinguish requests, which focus on the process, from demands, which focus on the outcome. In balanced communication, both partners commit to the process of expressing and listening to each other rather than solely attaching to a specific outcome.

Requests blossom from your ability to identify what you need and to ask for what would help satisfy that need. They can take the form of *action* requests or *connection* requests. An action request is asking your partner to do something (e.g., make the bed in the morning). A connection request is an invitation to relate (e.g., asking your partner to share how they feel or actively listen). Making requests can feel scary as it can lead to feeling shame or fear of being perceived as selfish or needy, but it is ultimately an act of vulnerability and courage. Each time you ask for what you need, you are creating an opening for intimacy in your relationship.

The way to master making and receiving requests is to practice, reflect, and refine, so let's practice requests using NVC.

Practice: PUTTING IT ALL TOGETHER

This is a joint discussion practice that should take about 20 to 30 minutes. Do this in a relaxing atmosphere where you both feel comfortable.

1. Together, choose a mildly challenging issue (e.g., a chore you'd like your partner to do more of) that isn't highly distressing for either of you.

2. One partner will attempt the NVC process while the other listens and responds. Use the following prompts, but allow the language to evolve to fit your speaking style:

   ◈ I observe . . .
   ◈ I feel . . .
   ◈ I need . . .
   ◈ I request . . .

3. Switch roles.

4. Discuss how it felt to be in different roles. What was challenging or easy?

If you become angry or want to blame your partner during the exercise, pause and use RAIN (see page 58) or breathing to re-center and identify feelings and needs.

The key to NVC is practice and refinement. The more you practice, the easier it will be to use in challenging moments. Now that you've practiced, let's review and refine the process. Here are a few additional notes on making requests:

- State requests clearly and positively. Focus on what you would like the person to do rather than what you would like them to *stop* doing.
- Make requests specific, concrete, and actionable. Break requests down into easily doable parts (e.g., "Could you wash the dishes before we go to bed tonight?" or "Could you listen to my perspective about this for five minutes?").
- Make requests, not demands. A request always allows for the other person to say no.

The difference between requests and demands is particularly important to highlight. We often feel that if we ask nicely, we are entitled to an affirmative response, but in reality, this is an expectation that puts unnecessary pressure on our partner and sets us up for disappointment. If we can ask for what we want without attachment to the outcome, this gives our partners freedom, helps them see our needs more clearly, and creates space for collaborative problem-solving.

Practice: ASKING WITHOUT ATTACHMENT

To ensure requests do not become demands, we must let go of our attachment to an outcome. Humor can be a great way to do this. This joint practice should take about 20 to 30 minutes. Do this in a relaxing atmosphere where you both feel comfortable. Set an intention to be creative and playful!

1. Choose an issue that has caused friction in your relationship. This can be either a *connection* request (e.g., asking for quality time together) or an *action* request (e.g., help with a chore or task), and use your new NVC skills to make this request of your partner.

2. Your partner will say no or decline your request in some way.

3. Rephrase the request at least five times in five different ways (play with words, body language, and tone of voice).

4. Your partner will decline the request using different words, emotional tone, body language, and tone of voice each time.

5. Switch roles.

Talk about what it felt like to hear no when making requests, and what stories arose about yourself, your partner, and your relationship. Note how you felt in response to the different tones and forms of no.

Variations: 1) Try the exercise with both connection and action requests and discuss how the experience changes. 2) Try this with yeses instead of nos, and discuss how the experience differs.

Learning to make requests that speak to our needs and do not have hidden strings attached allows new levels of self-expression, satisfaction, and intimacy. Practice making even small requests every day this week and watch what happens in your relationship.

Wrap-Up

◈ Feelings reveal underlying needs. Painful feelings often alert us to unmet needs.

◈ Healthy differentiation is essential for intimacy because it helps us manage anxiety, self-soothe, and meet our needs while in contact with our partners.

◈ Requests are different from demands in that they allow our partners the freedom to say no.

◈ Success in navigating our conflicts is not about agreeing but about being aware of and expressing our feelings and needs.

We are what we repeatedly do.
Excellence, then, is not an act,
but a habit.

—ARISTOTLE

SEVEN

Putting Your Practices to Work

TURNING PRACTICE INTO HABIT

With our natural tendencies to resist change, procrastinate, get distracted, or lose motivation, what is the secret to making new practices stick long enough to become habits? As discussed in chapter 3 (see page 41), habits are automatic responses to situations that we acquire through repetition. New habits can take up to eight months to build, so patience, practice, and dedication are essential. Think of the habits you are creating as seeds in your relationship garden. Rather than digging up the seeds to check on growth, simply keep watering and tending to the seeds and trust that consistent tending and the right conditions will lead to growth!

The first step is to create a plan to practice your new skills. Remember to choose exercises you enjoy to support your intrinsic motivation driven by internal feelings, like a greater sense of joy, rather than by external rewards, such as accolades. This is correlated with greater creativity and play, better understanding, and a stronger inclination to get back on track when we stray from our practice.

When scheduling, set realistic expectations for your practice, and be compassionate with yourself when you fall off track. Let go of the need to do the practices "right." Overall consistency is more important than perfection.

Planning

Now that you have experience with planning, adapt the planning process to best suit your needs. You can refer back to page 42 in chapter 3 if you need to review the steps again.

Now, take a moment to close your eyes and connect with your values. Call to mind a vision of your ideal relationship and ask what communication skills would support that vision over the next week, month, and year. Would you like to have frequent check-ins, make more requests, or improve your listening or assertiveness skills? Note what comes to mind.

Grab your journal and review the exercises. Keeping your values in mind, list your top three joint exercises from this part of the book and your top one or two solo exercises so far. Draw checkboxes to the right of the solo exercises so you can check them off once completed.

Review your solo exercises and get a sense of what days and times have natural breaks that would support consistent practice. Sit down with your partner and take turns sharing your top three exercises. Create a shared checklist of three to four joint exercises or rituals, and discuss how often you will do them.

Tracking Your Progress

Remember that tracking can increase happiness, satisfaction, and motivation. Acknowledging the work you and your partner are doing is as important as the work itself! Check in with yourself about how tracking has been going. What methods or strategies are you using? Which have fallen by the wayside and why?

The list of tools I recommended in chapter 3 (see page 43) are calendar tracking, journal tracking, and partner check-ins. Read over their descriptions, and reflect on whether these strategies are working or need to be adapted or reworked, or if you need to recommit to them.

If these strategies aren't working, brainstorm ideas that might work better for you. Consider starting a practice log or daily checklist in your journal or smartphone. Try a spreadsheet program, an app, or online platform to prompt your tracking. Get creative: Use stickers, emojis, colored pens, images, and vision boards, or create rewards for yourself.

If the partner check-ins aren't happening, consider ways to make these more fun and intrinsically motivating. For example, make a ritual out of pillow talk, and spend a few minutes each night acknowledging the progress and positive changes you've made in your relationship and personal lives.

If your motivation is flagging, ask yourself, "How can I make tracking fun?" and act on the answer you receive!

SETTING MUTUAL GOALS

Mutual goals are an important aspect of maintaining a relationship that is satisfying and fulfilling to both partners.

Through consistent and repeated small actions toward your mutual goals, you create a ripple effect in your relationship that looks and feels like a much bigger change than you expected. Try the following to gain clarity on your mutual relationship goals:

1. Grab some loose-leaf paper and pens.

2. On the page, draw a rectangle divided into four quadrants or a diamond. Each quadrant or point on the diamond represents one of four value domains: health, love, work, and play.

3. Discuss your shared relationship values in each area.

4. List these shared values in each of these domains on your drawing.

5. In a different color, write down a shared goal, aspiration, or intention for each of these four areas that you'd like to accomplish in the next five years, the next year, and the next six months.

6. Discuss specific actions you will each take toward meeting each of these goals.

7. Re-create a final draft and place it where you both can see it daily.

Let these mutual goals inform your commitment statements!

Commitment to Solo Practice

Since the goal here is for you to internalize the practices in this book in a way that feels personal and sustainable, I encourage you to adapt these commitment prompts to suit your needs if they didn't work the first time you used them.

Use or adapt the commitment statement on page 44 in chapter 3 to commit to a solo practice. Make sure the goal is SMART (specific, measurable, achievable, relevant, and time-bound).

Commitment to Joint Practice

With your partner, pick another exercise you can practice as a couple one to three times this week. Discuss how this exercise connects to your shared relationship values to increase your investment in this practice.

In your journals, write a shared commitment statement using your own adaptations of the prompt on page 45.

Create Your Weekly Practice Schedule

Grab your partner and your calendars. Set aside 20 minutes for this scheduling exercise. Make scheduling itself an opportunity for mindfulness by removing all distractions.

Sit comfortably beside each other, and set a timer for 20 minutes. Decide together how many weeks you will wait before you start the next part of the book, and look at the weeks ahead so that you can add the practices you've just committed to into your schedules.

Schedule in your joint practices first. Think about how you can rearrange your schedules, if necessary, so that you can prioritize time together for these practices. Next, schedule in the solo practices you will repeat over the coming weeks.

Set reminders and arrange "cues" (e.g., journals on your nightstand) to help you remember to practice.

CHECK-IN

Acknowledging and tracking your progress is integral to your sustained practice and therefore to your well-being and your relationship. After a week, check in as a couple and review how you have done with your goals this week. Honest reflection supports growth by helping us appreciate our progress, or notice, recalibrate, and recommit when we have fallen off track. Add a check-in date for a week from now to your calendars and set a reminder!

How Did You Do?

Review your practice lists and commitment statements. Check off practices you completed on your practice lists, and outwardly express appreciation to yourself and your partner for every practice you did. Review your journal reflections, and express appreciation for any changes you noticed in your behavior, your partner's behavior, or your relationship itself.

Nonjudgmentally note where you didn't meet your goals, and reflect on why this didn't happen. Whether due to flagging motivation, external circumstances, procrastination, or something else, be kind to yourself about getting off track. If you notice you are being self-critical, adjust your self-talk by compassionately cheerleading yourself the way you would a friend in the same situation. Note in your journal how you will adjust your practices or mindset to realign with your values and adjust your calendar accordingly.

Sticking with It

Remember that building new habits is a challenge that requires consistent practice, faith, and self-compassion. Getting off course is not failure, but simply a reminder to return to your intention. Instead of beating yourself up for mistakes, you can compassionately ask "What got in the way this time? How do I adjust?" and recommit to your plan from a place of new awareness and understanding.

Here's a quick list of tips to support you in sticking with your new practices:

◈ **Practice in a consistent time and place:** Research has shown that this supports habit formation (e.g., practicing first thing in the morning next to your bed).

◈ **Set a reminder:** Use calendar reminders, smartphone alerts, or text reminders. Here's a fun variation: Use an SMS scheduling app or your smartphone to schedule loving reminder texts to your partner (with their permission).

◈ **Use cues:** For example, set this book by your bed as a reminder to practice in the morning.

◈ **Create rewards:** Follow through on the rewards named in your commitment statements (e.g., a joint bubble bath after your evening meditation, a dinner date, or a couples massage) if you stick to 90 percent of the practices. Appreciation is also a wonderful reward!

◈ **Be compassionate with yourself and each other:** If you don't follow through on your commitments, be understanding, and start again!

◈ **Be appreciative:** Express appreciation for any progress you notice, no matter how small.

◈ **Accountability:** Keep up with your tracking, and enlist others to check in with you—your partner, friends, family, a therapist, or coach.

Remember, it's natural to wander off track, but the more support and accountability structures you provide for yourself, the easier it will be to reset when your motivation wanes.

I want this music, and this dawn,
and the warmth of your cheek
against mine.

—RUMI

PART THREE

Enhancing Intimacy

THE CHALLENGE

Our ability to be intimate with our partners is tried and tested as we wed, weather the challenges of family and daily life, endure sickness, have children, and become less able to hide our edges and difficult parts. As relationships progress and our individual lives become more entwined and interdependent, physical and emotional intimacy may be slowly replaced by problem-solving and to-do lists. We may not even notice that the spark of intimacy has waned until we wake up one day to find ourselves contemplating separation, looking outside our marriage for intimate connection, or simply thinking, "I'm unhappy, but this is just how life is."

Drew and Han came to therapy to restore intimacy in the tenth year of their marriage. Their second child had just turned three, and Drew had recently transitioned back into her career after years of focusing on motherhood. The couple had weathered a difficult infant illness with their first child, the onset of aging and illness in Han's dad, Han's stressful and travel-heavy career, and Drew's two severe bouts with postpartum anxiety and depression. Drew's transition back to work eased some financial strain, but it left her exhausted and less emotionally available. Drew and Han had become masterful at managing the day-to-day challenges of family life but felt more like business partners than a couple.

The chemistry and passion that had characterized the beginning of their relationship faded as the couple tackled the responsibilities of childrearing and gradually became habituated to their lives and each other.

THE REMEDY

Learning to bring open, curious attention to what we appreciate in our partners can help revive intimacy and passion in our relationship and see our shared lives with fresh eyes. Gratitude opens our hearts and has been shown in scientific studies to create a sense of well-being, regulate stress, improve sleep, reduce pain, and increase our sense of resilience. All these benefits help us show up in our relationships with more presence and joy, and they make space for our partners to do the same.

Practicing daily gratitude allowed Drew and Han to rediscover what they loved about each other and helped revive the chemistry and passion of their early days. The belief "this is just how marriage is" was replaced by effervescent feelings of appreciation and love that led to deepening emotional and physical intimacy.

Generosity of the heart is not measured by the number of presents or the cost of the bouquet. It's our generosity with our eyes, our listening, our kisses, our thoughtfulness . . . and the mementos we bring to our beloved.

—CHARLOTTE KASL, PHD
IF THE BUDDHA DATED

EIGHT

The Beauty of Gratitude

THE ENDLESS BENEFITS OF GRATITUDE

Our lives inevitably consist of a mixture of joys and sorrows, highs and lows, bitter moments and sweet ones. Mindfulness helps us weather these ups and downs with openness, curiosity, and nonjudgment. The quality of gratitude picks up where mindfulness leaves off and allows us to appreciate the beauty in life's difficult, happy, sad, and triumphant moments— because they are all equally a part of our one precious life.

One of the challenges we face as humans is that we have evolved to focus more on negative interactions and potential threats, as opposed to the positive things happening around us. In psychology, this is known as the *negativity bias* and has been evolutionarily adaptive in helping us survive and avoid danger. Practicing mindfulness counteracts the brain's negative tendencies by allowing us to cultivate a wider perspective, defuse from negative thoughts and stories, and choose where we place our focus. In this more mindful state, we can focus our attention on values and the cultivation of qualities like gratitude and compassion.

Gratitude is simply appreciation and thankfulness for that which is valuable and meaningful in our lives. It's often experienced in our hearts as a warm, opening sensation. Cultivating gratitude strengthens the parts of the brain that regulate stress, sleep, eating, and learning, allowing us to show up feeling happier, more satisfied, more motivated, and more connected in our relationships. Research shows that expressing and receiving gratitude supports forgiveness, conflict resolution, relationship satisfaction, and mutual thoughtfulness and caretaking behaviors among partners.

When Mandy and Jamal came to therapy, Mandy was on the verge of ending the relationship over Jamal's substance use and her fear that "things would never change." After several months of Jamal's sobriety and the couple practicing mindfulness and communication skills, they began doing gratitude meditations and rituals together. They started a bedtime ritual of sharing their gratitude, noting that they felt closer and happier than ever before. In their last session, Mandy tearfully shared how grateful she felt for Jamal and his sobriety, and how she felt in her heart that Jamal was living up to the potential she had always known he had. Jamal shared his gratitude for his new awareness about how to "show up better" for Mandy.

Like mindfulness, gratitude's benefits come from regular practice, so as you do the practices to follow, think of ways to incorporate them into your daily life. I recommend practicing gratitude just before bed as this has been shown to decrease negative thoughts and improve sleep.

The following practice is intended to open your heart to the feeling of gratitude. Practicing this technique can help calm your nervous system and slow your heart rate during conflict.

Practice: GRATITUDE DROP-IN

This joint practice should take 5 to 10 minutes plus a few minutes for discussion. Do this preferably before bed each night this week. You can also do this as a solo practice.

1. Lie in a comfortable position.

2. Facing your partner, close your eyes, and focus your attention on the center of your chest around your heart.

3. Breathe slowly and deeply at a comfortable pace into your heart center.

4. Call to mind a quality or characteristic in your partner or your relationship that you deeply appreciate, and let your focus rest here for several minutes.

5. Open your eyes when you feel ready, and hold eye contact with your partner for several minutes, noticing physical sensations in your heart center.

6. Take turns sharing your experience with your partner.

Using your journal, spend a few extra moments reflecting on what gratitude feels like in your body.

In addition to cultivating gratitude through meditation practice, it can be useful to expand our awareness of gratitude to the present moment. The next practice is designed to help you shift your survival-oriented negativity bias by bringing your focus to savoring, appreciating, and experiencing gratitude in your day-to-day life.

Practice: THE GRATITUDE BIAS

For this joint exercise, set the intention in the morning to practice bringing your awareness to gratitude throughout the day. In the evening before bed, discuss your experience.

1. Observe each moment of gratitude and appreciation today, bringing awareness to every "thank you" you say and joyful feeling you experience.

2. In these moments, pause. Notice if you feel present and attentive, or stressed and absentminded.

3. Notice sensations or feelings in your chest or body. See if you can expand the feeling of gratitude by amplifying the physical sensations of it and naming to yourself exactly what you feel grateful for.

4. If it feels right, express your appreciation from this heartfelt place of awareness or say, "Thank you." (If you've already said it, feel free to say it again!)

Before bed, review these sensory experiences of gratitude with your partner to expand your appreciative feelings, bring you closer to each other, and support your gratitude practice!

EVERYDAY GRATITUDE PRACTICE

Gratitude can improve your relationship, deepen intimacy, and maintain relationship bonds with your partner, but only with dedicated practice over time. A study discussed in *Greater Good Magazine* that involved writing weekly gratitude letters showed that the mental health benefits of gratitude gradually increased over time. The study noted some benefit at four weeks, but more significant improvements appeared after 12 weeks of practice. For this reason, it's useful to focus on bringing the practice and expression of gratitude into your everyday life as a habit rather than attempting to use gratitude as a fix-it or tool to achieve an immediate desired outcome. In addition to benefitting the mental health of the person expressing gratitude, a study at Kent State University showed that recipients of letters of gratitude consistently felt happier than the letter writer anticipated.

Some of the couples I work with practice cultivating everyday gratitude through meditation or rituals, whereas others prefer to incorporate small gestures and words of appreciation into their daily life. Sometimes, one partner prefers a meditation or ritual whereas the other prefers to focus on words or gestures of appreciation. In my opinion, the most important part of any gratitude practice is to enjoy it while you do it to make it sustainable!

After a rocky start in their relationship, Kevin and Roya began focusing on developing a foundation of trust and security in the therapy sessions. Kevin noticed that practicing "Gratitude Drop-In" (see page 114) with Roya—as well as the next practice, "Picture Memories"—helped him soothe his anxiety in moments when he felt triggered to shut down, such as when he felt his needs weren't being met. After a few months of daily gratitude journaling and sharing gratitude before bed, Kevin reported that he experienced fewer instances of wanting to shut down or pull away, and more comfort and joy being close to Roya.

In the Netflix special *Brené Brown: A Call to Courage*, Brown mentions how her daughter took a "picture memory" by closing her eyes and using her senses to remember a joy-filled moment. Your own picture memories can be a resource to call upon in moments of conflict or stress and can be done together with your partner to increase connectedness and enhance shared experiences.

This practice builds on the previous exercise of observing moments of gratitude. You can take "picture memories" when spontaneous feelings of gratitude arise—on your own or ask your partner to do it with you. You can also do this as a joint practice after meditation or in place of it. When you feel deep gratitude in your heart, let the moment in with all your senses.

1. Wherever you are, observe with your eyes at least five specific objects you see.

2. Close your eyes to experience the moment with your other senses. Notice at least four things you hear, three things you sense through touch, two things you smell, and one thing you taste.

3. Quickly scan your body to notice what you feel.

4. Place your awareness in your heart, and imagine all the sensory input of this "snapshot" being imprinted there.

By taking picture memories, you can enhance your awareness of joyful memories your heart records, thus increasing your awareness, enhancing your gratitude and enjoyment, and bolstering your relationship.

The daily practices of writing and expressing your appreciation are helpful for sustaining your focus on gratitude. Writing about gratitude in the morning primes us to notice positive experiences throughout the day, and reflecting at night helps soothe us and calm our nerves before bed.

This twice daily practice can be done solo or alongside your partner. It only takes about 5 minutes in the morning and evening, and requires your journal.

1. In the morning, list the following in your journal:

   ◈ Three things you are grateful for in your relationship. These can be actions your partner takes or inherent qualities you are grateful for in your partner. These can be seemingly small such as the smell of your partner's shampoo, or deep abiding qualities like their strength of character. It can be about the relationship itself such as a shared love of music.

⬦ One gesture, phrase, or action you can take to show your appreciation.

⬦ One joyful thing you can savor (something you'll do for sheer pleasure).

2. In the evening, list the following in your journal:

⬦ Three things that happened in your relationship or qualities in your partner you are grateful for.

Gratitude is best expressed, so share at least one item from your gratitude list with your partner before bed. Sharing will help you stay motivated and make the practice more intrinsically gratifying.

GRATITUDE FOR YOUR PARTNER

Acknowledgment is a universal human need, and expressing gratitude for our partners is a form of deep acknowledgment. Outwardly expressing gratitude in your relationship, rather than simply thinking or feeling it, was shown in a study published in *Personal Relationships* to increase desire to give unconditionally in the relationship. In this study, participants saw the relationship in a new light—as one in which they were there to support and help each other without expectation of a return. This didn't happen from simply thinking about being grateful. The exercises in this section involve a reflection component, but the important takeaway is to share your appreciation with your partner after each exercise and reflection.

The power of deep acknowledgment and appreciation emerged in a session with Ling and Trent. Trent explained to Ling that her lack of deep connection with his family was difficult for him. Ling argued that Trent didn't understand her perspective, because *his* relationship with *her* family was easy. Trent explained that his connection with her family only appeared easy because of hard work and effort on his part to build those relationships.

We paused the interaction, and I asked Ling if she'd noticed Trent's efforts to go out of the way to be kind to her family. Ling realized that she had taken Trent's social skills and effort with her family for granted, and her face softened. She looked at Trent and said, "I appreciate your efforts to be close to my family." She looked at me and said, "Thank you," and then looked back at Trent, smiled, and reached across the couch to touch his cheek and said, "I love you." Trent looked relieved and happy to receive acknowledgment for a core part of his personality and for his intentional effort to make Ling happy.

Practice: GRATITUDE LOVE LISTS

This joint exercise is designed to excavate and highlight what you love about your partner and to practice expressing the unacknowledged gifts you each bring to your partnership. It should take about 10 minutes and requires your journals.

1. In your journal, list five big things you are grateful for in your partner (e.g., qualities like their loyalty, health, integrity, etc.).

2. Next, list five small things you generally overlook that you appreciate (e.g., their eyelashes, the way they buy you popcorn at the movies, any unique quirks or imperfections you appreciate, etc.).

3. Share the items on your gratitude love lists with each other, one list a time. The person listening can focus on receiving the words with their heart, and the person giving can focus on the feeling of sharing from their heart.

This practice lays the groundwork for some of the upcoming practices that will help support your relationship itself.

GO DEEPER
Shared Gratitude List

To further strengthen your appreciation for each other, create a gratitude list of your relationship together! Grab your journals for this joint exercise, which should take about 20 minutes.

1. Close your eyes, and do a 3-minute Gratitude Drop-In (see page 114).

2. In your journals, individually brainstorm every little thing you are grateful for in your relationship. Consider values, lifestyle habits, memories, plans, rituals, inside jokes, and qualities; the more obscure and unique, the better.

3. Take turns sharing items on your lists.

4. As you share, write each item down on a fresh piece of loose-leaf paper to create your shared gratitude list.

5. Place the list where you can both see it regularly as a reminder of your appreciation.

When you are done, give each other a hug and express gratitude and love for your partner as they are right now.

Just as we can often take our partners' gifts for granted, sometimes we forget what we love about ourselves and all the little, unseen, or unspoken ways in which our partners support these parts of ourselves. The following practice is designed to help us fill our own gratitude cup and highlight the ways our partners honor and support us.

Practice: SELF-APPRECIATION

This practice, which can be done solo or alongside your partner, is adapted from the work of Kristin Neff, PhD, and Christopher Germer, PhD. It should take about 10 minutes and requires your journal.

1. Get comfortable, and close your eyes.

2. Call to mind four qualities you like about yourself as a person and four qualities you like about yourself as a partner. Choose one of these qualities to focus on.

3. Bring to mind all the ways, seen and unseen, that your partner supports you in bringing out this quality.

4. Open your eyes when you're ready.

5. In your journal, write about how your partner supports the qualities you like about yourself. Also, reflect on how you react to compliments about these qualities. Perhaps you receive them graciously, or maybe you resist, avoid, or dismiss them. Is receiving appreciation comfortable or uncomfortable? Why?

After both partners have done this exercise, share your takeaways. You chose each other for a reason. Taking time to reflect on how you bring out the best in each other and how you give and receive appreciation are essential parts of gratitude.

GRATITUDE FOR YOUR RELATIONSHIP

As discussed earlier, relationships have their own cycles, dynamics, and patterns. Once we recognize our cycles and step back from automatic reactions and patterns, gratitude becomes a powerful tool to enrich, grow, and deepen our relationships. Regularly including gratitude practices such as thoughtful gestures can positively impact your relationship cycle.

According to a study discussed in *Greater Good Magazine*, regular thoughtful gestures increase feelings of gratitude and indebtedness and contribute to a perception of greater relationship quality by both partners. Another study discussed in the same publication showed "relationship maintenance" behaviors, such as motivation to reciprocate thoughtful gestures, improved when a spouse responded to gestures of gratitude. When practiced regularly, these reciprocal, thoughtful gestures led to a self-reinforcing positive cycle characterized by gratitude and caring behaviors.

In Jamal and Mandy's last session, the couple was able to recognize and express their appreciation for the efforts, big and small, that each partner had made to change their relationship cycle. Mandy noted that when she practiced being mindful, she saw how Jamal was making his own improvements to his health even though these improvements looked different from what Mandy would have expected. Jamal noted he could now see Mandy's efforts to calm herself before nagging him. Mandy shared that the relationship felt good in a deeper way than ever before.

Both partners took time to reflect on how their unique love story evolved, made promises to continually recommit to their practices (sobriety for Jamal and mindfulness of anxiety for Mandy), and discussed how they would return to these practices or seek out therapy again if their cycle of conflict started to spiral.

Practice: GESTURES OF APPRECIATION

Sometimes it's easy to know what thoughtful gestures your partner appreciates, and sometimes it's less obvious. Take about 10 minutes to do this joint exercise to discover what makes each of you feel appreciated. Grab your journals and get comfortable.

1. In your journal, list 5 to 10 actions, big and small, your partner can do or already does to show you they appreciate you (e.g., writing notes, sending thankful texts, washing your car, giving you compliments or flowers, etc.). Focus on specific gestures and not inherent qualities like "kindness."

2. Take turns sharing your lists with each other.

3. After sharing, make a note in your journal of at least two gestures you will make to show your appreciation for your partner this week. You do not need to share these with your partner now.

4. Make a note to yourself about how you can be receptive when your partner expresses appreciation to you.

Being receptive to thoughtful gestures is as important as the gesture itself, so remember to share your gratitude for something your partner has done. If you forget in the moment, share at bedtime when you're reflecting on your day.

In addition to focusing on day-to-day gratitude, it can help to take a bird's-eye view of your overall relationship and cycle and to appreciate the ways in which you have woven a beautiful tapestry of connection that can hold you together when times are difficult.

Like wine, the love in your relationship deepens and matures with age. There is a beautiful wedding tradition attributed to the Dutch in which the bride and groom stow love letters and a special bottle of wine in a wooden box. The couple is not to open the box until a predetermined future date (such as a tenth anniversary) unless they encounter difficulty in their relationship, at which point they can open the box.

When the couple opens the box, they read their letters and drink the wine together. In this tradition, drinking the wine represents taking in the complex bitter and sweet aspects of life and the letters represent the love and appreciation that is the foundation of the relationship. The following practice is adapted from that ritual.

Practice: DUTCH WINE BOX TRADITION

Choose a box and stationery together for this practice. Decide if you will use a bottle of wine or a different symbolic object to represent your connection over time. You can do this exercise to mark a special occasion or simply as a gratitude ritual. The letter writing practice should take about an hour to complete, and each partner can write the letter on their own.

1. Together, choose a future date to open the box, agreeing that if you face difficulties before this point, you may decide to open the box sooner.

2. Set aside time away from distractions to write a letter from your heart to your partner about your relationship. Set the ambience by lighting a candle.

3. Close your eyes and spend some time reflecting on your relationship from the moment you met until this moment, allowing memories to arise in succession.

4. Open your eyes and write the letter, describing the qualities you love about your partner, the reasons you fell in love with them, and your commitment to and intentions for the relationship.

5. Place the letter in a sealed envelope.

6. When you have both written your letters, place them in the box along with the bottle of wine or symbolic object. Store the box in a safe place.

7. When you open the box on the designated date, read the letters and share the wine or object.

This practice builds your reservoirs of gratitude and creates a time capsule of your appreciation and love for each other that you can return to when needed.

Gratitude is easy to feel when we are in love, but it can be harder to access in times of struggle. By focusing on gratitude for your relationship as a whole, you strengthen the bonds between you and your partner and build and rebuild a foundation of trust, appreciation, and kindness between you.

Wrap-Up

◈ Gratitude practices direct our attention to appreciation for every-day moments and to unique qualities that our partners and our relationships possess.

◈ Cultivating gratitude helps us balance our natural negativity bias, and be a more loving, forgiving, and generous partners.

◈ Expressing our gratitude expands its benefits to our relationship, and sharing gratitude before bed can even improve sleep.

We can amplify gratitude by noticing how it feels in our bodies, taking "picture memories," writing it down, making thoughtful gestures, and expressing it to our partners.

Our longing is also our desire to be known completely. Imagine having your beloved look tenderly into your eyes, knowing all your secrets, having seen you be crabby and sweet, selfish and generous, and still truly love you. Imagine being able to do the same. This is the potential of a conscious relationship.

—CHARLOTTE KASL, PHD
IF THE BUDDHA DATED

NINE

The Role of Gratitude in Intimacy

SEEING YOUR PARTNER WITH FRESH EYES

In most long-term relationships, it's easy to get caught up in the day-to-day grind and lose sight of the wonderful things about your partner that first sparked excitement in your courtship. Mindfulness helps expand your awareness, and gratitude practice directs your attention to the unique attributes you appreciate in your partner. In this chapter, you'll learn how cultivating gratitude, compassion, and vulnerability can help you see your partner with fresh eyes and deepen your intimacy.

Intimacy is a deep and close familiarity with another person. It's a part of romantic connection, but it's about more than romance. It's about being able to unmask ourselves in front of another—to be received, welcomed, and cared for, exactly as we are. Sometimes we avoid intimacy because we fear losing ourselves or being rejected; we are uncomfortable with imperfection; or perhaps the vulnerability intimacy requires elicits feelings of weakness or fear, or memories of past trauma or violation. But intimacy flourishes when we have the courage to meet these feelings in ourselves and receive our partners as they are—flaws and all.

To do this, we must first create an environment of safety in our relationship by cultivating empathy and compassion, both of which require our willingness to show up, be honest, and face uncomfortable feelings. Whereas empathy is the ability to deeply understand the feelings of another, compassion is the ability to feel care for and extend benevolence to others when they are suffering. Many meditation traditions teach the cultivation of compassion as part of spiritual practice.

Extending compassion toward ourselves and others reduces feelings of criticism and judgment, generates feelings of connection, calms our bodies, and allows us to stay in a place of caregiving rather than in a posture of defense. Compassion primes our minds to take in more positive information, allowing us to focus on those attributes we appreciate in our partners.

Giving compassion activates the same pleasure centers that register sex, money, and chocolate in both the giver and receiver, leading to enhanced feelings of intimacy. Studies have shown that being self-compassionate is a stronger predictor of healthy relationships than self-esteem or even attachment style. The good news is that there are simple ways we can cultivate and practice compassion.

Practice: GENERATING COMPASSION

In this solo exercise, you will spend some time giving yourself gestures of self-compassion. Mindful self-compassion practice, developed by Kristin Neff, PhD, and Christopher Germer, PhD, teaches three main skills by which people can practice cultivating compassion for themselves. Read through the descriptions of these skills, and then spend some time practicing each one.

Warmth: This includes physical warmth such as a warm fire, a blanket, or a cup of tea, as well as emotional warmth and a warm tone of voice, like the tone you'd use to say, "Good morning" after a full night's rest and excitement to greet the day and your partner.

Gentle touch: Gestures like a hand over the heart, a caress of the face, and massaging or rubbing a forearm or knee can trigger the release of oxytocin and produce feelings of warmth and pleasure.

Soothing vocalizations: Use a warm soothing tone to talk kindly and use affectionate pet names like "dear" or supportive phrases such as, "I see you're hurting." "Aww" is the universal sound of compassion.

Notice how you feel when receiving these gestures of self-compassion. It may feel a little strange at first! In your journal, write down some ways you can incorporate each of these self-compassion gestures into your life this week. Then list three actions you will take to show compassion toward your partner, and commit to them.

Another way of seeing our partners with fresh eyes is to attune to them with compassion. When we attune to our partners, mirror neurons in our brain fire in response to their words, feelings, and actions. These neurons generate a "felt experience" in our bodies that mirrors our partners' experiences. This "empathic resonance" can create feelings of intimacy—and, occasionally, it can lead to feeling overwhelmed and a desire to "fix" or reject our partners' feelings if they are painful or hard for us to accept. Compassion is a way to stay connected to ourselves and remain open and accepting of both the good and bad feelings our partners feel.

To receive our partners with care, even when we feel our hearts wanting to withdraw in fear, is an act of intimacy and one of the greatest gifts we can give them and our relationship. The following practice is designed to help you lovingly witness your partner while engaging compassion.

Practice: COMPASSIONATE BREATH

This is a joint exercise that can take anywhere from 5 to 20 minutes. As you do the exercise, allow yourself to accept whatever feelings arise in you as you practice compassionately witnessing your partner.

1. Set a timer for the length of time you wish to practice.

2. Sitting comfortably across from each other, soften your gaze, and receive your partner with warmth and a feeling of an inner smile.

3. Drop your awareness into the center of your chest and notice your heartbeat.

4. Cultivate a feeling of compassion in your heart, the feeling you would extend to a puppy that just tumbled down a flight of stairs.

5. Synchronize the rhythm of your breath with your partner's breath, inhaling as your partner exhales.

6. With each inhale, breathe your partner in with compassion. Imagine you are breathing in all their edges, their pain, and their defenses, as well as their joy.

7. With each exhale, allow yourself to let go, soften, and release all hardness, tension, and defenses, so that your partner can breathe you in with compassion.

8. Notice if you want to resist or defend in any way. Just for now, intend to soften, allow, and release your resistance.

9. When the timer rings, notice how you feel in your body.

Variations: 1) Practice this exercise lying down and touching or hugging. 2) Practice using affection or appreciation instead of compassion as your focus, and notice how your experience changes.

Seeing your partner clearly requires letting go of judgments, criticisms, ideas of right and wrong, and desires to appear "together" or perfect. This can be scary and vulnerable, but it allows us to connect in new and spontaneous ways and experience the deep, connected, and nourishing feelings of intimacy.

Brené Brown defines "vulnerability" as the courage to be yourself, noting that to be vulnerable necessarily involves "uncertainty, risk, and emotional exposure." As a society, we have been falsely taught that vulnerability is weakness and that perfection, achievement, and fearlessness are signs of strength. We've learned to judge ourselves and others when we fall short of these unrealistic expectations. This self-criticism prevents the expression of vulnerability and, in so doing, undermines our universal needs for belonging, connection, and intimacy. This shows up in subtle ways. For instance, one partner shares a feeling of disappointment or sadness, and the other partner offers a fix-it solution; or one partner opens up about their feelings, and the other recoils, withdraws in fear, or tells their partner to toughen up.

Think about the people you admire most: grandparents, children, celebrities, speakers, friends, your partner, and so on. Do you admire them because they are perfect? Or do you admire them for their unique qualities, like courage, genuineness, generosity, or integrity? It is inspiring to be in the presence of authentic expression. Furthermore, it feels comforting and safe: Studies show that honest and vulnerable communication calms the nervous system and decreases blood pressure and emotional reactivity in the person expressing, as well as in the person listening.

Embodying this kind of authentic expression requires us to embrace our imperfection. Vulnerability, like intimacy itself, is messy and imperfect and cannot be predicted, planned, or controlled. To experience it, we must lay down our defenses and bare ourselves to another with openness to whatever arises.

NURTURING INTIMACY WITH YOURSELF

Acceptance of others begins with self-acceptance. When we accept our feelings, needs, and flaws, we are able to expand our capacity to receive our partners as they are and create an opening in our relationship for new ways of relating to each other.

My client Risa identified strongly with her work as a lawyer. Her company's culture was to work long hours and never say no, which triggered Risa's perfectionist tendencies. Over time, her stress levels escalated, and her relationship with her husband, Stavros, eroded. She charged through every day at work and drank alcohol in the evenings to unwind, yet she felt increasingly distant from Stavros and from the version of herself she had been when they first married.

Risa started individual therapy, where she learned to recognize and express her own needs, feelings, and boundaries at work and in her marriage. She learned to soothe herself when stressed or plagued by low self-esteem and self-criticism with mindfulness and compassion rather than with alcohol. As a result, she began to convey more empathy, compassion, and gratitude to her family and to attune to her husband and relationship in a new way. Eventually, she even found a new job that better fit her needs. By developing intimacy with herself, Risa's marriage and life began to change.

Intimacy with yourself starts with awareness of your needs and feelings and continues with acceptance of all parts of yourself, including the parts you'd rather not face. When we can be intimate with ourselves, we exude peaceful confidence and are available to accept other people more fully.

The following guided visualization is designed to help you lovingly accept the parts of yourself you'd rather push away or criticize.

Practice: ACCEPTING ALL OF YOURSELF

This solo meditation can be practiced daily for 5, 10, or 15 minutes. You can work with as many parts of yourself as you would like.

1. Set a timer. Sit comfortably, close your eyes, and take several deep breaths.

2. Drop your awareness to the center of your chest near your heart.

3. Visualize a rosebud with its petals closed tightly in your heart center.

4. Bring your awareness to your breath. With each inhalation, unfold a petal of this rosebud. Let each unfolding petal peel away a difficult or painful memory, or a physical feeling of tension, pain, or being stuck. Open into each physical and emotional feeling as you inhale a petal open.

5. Call to mind a part of you that brings up feelings of shame or embarrassment. Perhaps this part has taken actions you aren't proud of; perhaps this part is anxious, reactive, or shuts down and avoids or hurts others. This may be a part you associate with a certain age (e.g., your teenage self) or quality (e.g., your stubborn self, perfectionist self, or avoidant self).

6. In your mind's eye, see this part of yourself before you.

7. In the open center of your heart, cultivate the feeling of loving compassion you would extend to a person you deeply love who is suffering or an animal that has gotten hurt.

8. Feeling this warm energy of compassion in the center of the rose (in your heart center), breathe in and lovingly accept this part of you with all of its suffering and difficult emotions.

9. On the out breath, imagine exhaling bright white light. Imagine the rose is there to assist you in processing the difficult emotions you

feel, acting like a plant taking in carbon dioxide and releasing oxygen, as it absorbs the difficult feelings and expels them transformed.

10. When the timer rings, conclude the receiving practice. Take several breaths, gently open your eyes, and notice how you feel.

Spend a few minutes writing in your journal about any sensations and emotions that arose. Pay attention this week to when similar emotions arise. You may be more conscious of and able to articulate them. You may also feel more comfortable expressing them. Use this practice regularly to develop more self-acceptance.

When we more fully accept ourselves, we become more aware of our boundaries, which is essential to nurturing intimacy with ourselves and our partners. A boundary is an emotional and energetic line that defines your values, ideals, desires, and needs. It can be felt physiologically through bodily signals indicating what you do and do not like or want.

Nurturing intimacy with yourself requires that you begin to tune in when your body and mind say yes and when they say no. Listening to and expressing your boundaries lets you be seen and understood by your partner, feel greater trust with yourself and your partner, and creates a foundation for emotional and physical intimacy.

Practice: BOUNDARIES—YES AND NO

This solo two-part exercise requires your journal. Set aside some time for yourself and get comfortable. Take as much time as you need.

Part 1: We often deny ourselves pleasure for fear of being indulgent, which can leave us feeling unfulfilled and drained. Tuning in to what feels pleasurable can help you find your full-bodied sense of yes.

1. In your journal, brainstorm a list of big pleasures and a list of small pleasures. Small pleasures are things you can do every day, like sticking your toes in the grass, a hand massage, and other sensual activities like sex or a nice dinner. Big pleasures are things you have to plan for the future, such as a balloon ride or an exotic vacation.

2. Schedule a day to go on a "pleasure diet." Make your intention for the day to pursue and truly receive the experience of deep feelings of pleasure that arise from engaging your senses, meeting your needs, and relaxing. If it brings you pleasure, then do it!

Part 2: Sometimes it can be hard to own our "no" in fear that it will jeopardize our connection with someone. In truth, when you say no to something that doesn't feel right, you are saying yes to yourself and defining your boundaries. Tune in to your "no":

1. In your journal, make a list of items, both big and small, that evoke a "no" response in you. Aversive or bothered reactions to something or a request may signal you are feeling a "no." Small items might include an aversion to tomatoes and big items might be if someone doesn't follow through on what they said they would do.

2. Throughout the week, bring your awareness to what you say no to and what you would like to say no to. At the end of each day, add to your list to bring more awareness to your "no" so you can start exercising it.

When you articulate and own your boundaries, you become more self-reliant and simultaneously more available to be present for others.

Being in a relationship implies interdependence, and cultivating emotional intimacy requires the courage to express the full range of your needs and feelings, despite the painful possibility that these might be denied or rejected.

EMOTIONAL INTIMACY

To experience connectedness through sex and physical intimacy, we must accept and welcome the full range of our emotions. Emotional intimacy is enhanced by our ability to be kind and compassionate, and to respect our boundaries and those of our partner and the relationship we have created. Commitment is one such boundary, as is setting aside protected time for rituals, dates, and even activities like going through this book together. Having a protected boundary creates a container in which intimacy can develop.

In his book *Wired for Love*, Stan Tatkin, PsyD, calls this safe zone or boundary around the relationship the "couple bubble," which he defines as a "mutually constructed membrane, cocoon, or womb, that holds the couple together and protects each partner from outside elements." To create this safe zone, both partners must agree that their partner's needs and well-being are a top priority.

When Stavros and Risa started couples therapy, each felt they didn't have a teammate anymore. Stavros felt isolated when they attended events and Risa talked to everyone else at the event, leaving him to fend for himself. Risa felt unimportant when Stavros allowed his mother to undermine Risa's parenting rules for their daughter and when Stavros would disagree with Risa in front of their daughter.

After making a shared couple agreement, Risa committed to spending at least half of the time at parties with Stavros and to check in with him periodically by physically standing near him and touching his arm in a gesture of support. Stavros agreed that he would reinforce Risa's household rules when his mother babysat and that he would set aside time to talk to Risa privately rather than disagreeing with her in front of their daughter. The couple began to feel a stronger sense of kinship and collaboration, even when they disagreed.

Practice: YOUR COUPLE AGREEMENT (OR "BAE AREA")

This joint exercise should take about 20 minutes. It will support you in collaboratively defining what boundaries would help you each feel important and valued. One of my clients from the Bay Area creatively titled this exercise "Bae Area," which seems appropriate! So grab your journals and get started.

1. Sit comfortably across from each other.

2. Together, name a recent or recurring difficult dynamic or conflict.

3. Close your eyes and individually reflect on what you would need from your partner to feel safe and be vulnerable in your relationship the next time this tension occurs.

4. Spend a few minutes writing about these needs in your journal.

5. Take turns sharing and discussing these needs.

6. Agree on one or two commitments you will make to take each other's needs into account and prioritize your relationship.

7. Set a future date to check in about how this practice has gone and to readjust or reaffirm the boundaries. Celebrate if you see improvement in your dynamic, and simply readjust your "Bae Area" lines if you do not.

Another way to enhance emotional intimacy is through regularly expressing your love to each other. As Buddhist monk Thich Nhat Hanh teaches, to properly love another person, you must "train" yourself by practicing being present and expressing love. He describes four aspects of love that one must be able to express: freedom, presence, holding another's sorrow, and vulnerability. Cultivating these qualities generate intimacy by teaching us to intentionally give love to ourselves rather than looking to someone to provide love for us.

Thich Nhat Hanh teaches simple mantras that evoke these qualities in the listener. In the following exercise, you will practice sharing these mantras with your partner.

Practice: MANTRAS FOR TRUE LOVE

This is a joint exercise. Allow 10 minutes for speaking and 10 minutes for reflections. Decide which partner will speak and which partner will receive first. The mantras included in this exercise are based on Thich Nhat Hanh's original phrases.

1. Sit comfortably, and together, inhale and exhale five times into your heart center to unite with the breath, inhaling presence and exhaling tension.

2. When the speaker feels aligned and centered, they will speak the following mantras from a heartfelt place, speaking slowly and pausing between phrases.

   - Do you have space in your heart and all around you?
   - I know that you are here, and it makes me happy.
   - You are really here, and I am glad about it.
   - I know that you suffer, and that is why I'm here for you.
   - Sometimes I suffer. Please help.

After you have completed the initial phrases, experiment with simpler phrases such as:

   - I'm with you.
   - I see you.
   - I accept you.
   - I forgive you.
   - I'm here for you.

3. The listener can pay attention to how they feel when each phrase is spoken, with eyes open or closed, and may jot notes in their journal between phrases.

4. When you've finished sharing these mantras, discuss together how the process felt. Let the listener speak first. Which phrases resonated? How did it feel mentally, physically, and emotionally to receive each phrase? Which ones are familiar and which ones would be nice to hear more of? Share phrases that resonated and led you to feel safe, seen, and understood, or create a phrase that would resonate with you and share it.

5. Switch roles and repeat this exercise either now or at a later time.

I recommend that you exchange these mantras with each other regularly as part of your bedtime ritual. Studies show that the happiest couples engage in meaningful pillow talk before going to sleep.

GO DEEPER
Sexual Fantasies

To deepen your emotional intimacy with each other, set aside some time to discuss your sexual fantasies. Sharing your unique fantasies can feel vulnerable, so allow for this vulnerability.

Take turns sharing fantasies you've had or what you imagine would feel good. If you need to stimulate your imagination, do an internet search for "sexual fantasies" or pick out a book such as *The Joy of Sex* by Alex Comfort, MD, and read it together.

If it feels difficult to talk openly, purchase a stack of index cards. Write one fantasy per card and exchange stacks with your partner. Take turns reading each other's fantasies aloud.

After you've done this exercise, commit to trying at least one new thing that each of you shared. Then, take a few moments to write in your journals how it felt to share these fantasies with your partner.

PHYSICAL INTIMACY

Oftentimes, emotional intimacy fosters deeper physical intimacy and is a great way to kick-start your sex life. Cultivating mindful awareness, nonjudgment, and listening skills engages your senses and deepens your connection to your own and your partner's body during lovemaking.

Mindful sex is about holding the sexual experience with open, curious, and playful attention, and not being afraid to reveal ourselves. If we become caught up in or distracted by thoughts and stories about the day, fantasies, or anxieties, we miss out on the nourishing experience of intimate connection. We resist intimacy for a number of reasons: Maybe we fear rejection, or maybe a history of childhood mistreatment leaves us guarded. These fears and anxieties are not just experienced psychologically but physiologically as well.

Kevin and Roya's relationship, for instance, suffered from Kevin's early-life abuse. Growing up with a verbally abusive mother, Kevin had learned at a young age that emotional intimacy was threatening. To avoid criticism, he had protected himself by performing as demanded, all the while dissociating from his body and traveling elsewhere in his mind. During sex with Roya, Kevin would become overwhelmed and conflicted. He had found it easier to sleep with women he did not have strong feelings for. When he had sex with Roya, Kevin would dissociate physically and mentally. Afterward, he would shut down. He cared deeply for Roya, but during sex, he felt a mixture of shame, abandonment, and rejection that he otherwise didn't experience and couldn't quite name, prompting him to withdraw.

In therapy, we practiced building emotional and physical intimacy in small increments and in the presence of compassion to build Kevin's ability to stay in his body when experiencing strong emotions. Kevin learned to let go of his inner critic and focus on the emotions, breath, and physical sensations arising in the moment.

If we can stay compassionate with ourselves and our partners, we activate our relaxation response and release the bonding hormone oxytocin (rather than the fight-or-flight hormone cortisol), thereby enhancing our ability to experience intimacy. The following exercise is designed to help you practice compassion and self-soothing, let go of the need to perform, bond deeply with your partner, and mindfully witness your emotions, breath, and sensations in the moment.

This 40-minute joint intimacy exercise is nonsexual and is done with clothing on. This creates a safe space for both partners to fully witness feelings that arise. Stop if either partner feels overwhelmed at any point in the practice.

1. Decide who will receive first, and set a timer for 20 minutes.

2. Lie in a comfortable position, and close your eyes. Take several deep breaths. Scan your body head to toe, relaxing each body part as you scan. Silently label thoughts as they arise, and let them go.

3. Name emotions that are present. Use RAIN (see page 58) to recognize, allow, investigate, and nurture emotions with gratitude and loving acceptance.

4. Cultivate a feeling of loving-kindness, feeling this for yourself and your partner. Feel it in your heart as a feeling of love and warmth, and infuse your breath with this feeling.

5. When you have cultivated this feeling, signal to your partner that you are ready by placing a hand over your heart.

6. Your partner now explores your clothed body with nonsexual caressing and touch (e.g., caressing or touching your face, hands, hair, back, etc.). As they do so, allow and notice whatever feelings, sensations, and thoughts arise in you.

7. When the timer rings, switch roles, and set the timer for another 20 minutes.

Discuss with your partner how it felt to receive and how it felt to explore in this nonsexual and gentle way. Did you discover anything new about your partner? Yourself?

In addition to cultivating compassion, facing both the pleasurable feelings and the wounds stored in our physical bodies requires that we approach our body and our partners' bodies with openness, mindfulness, trust, and respect.

The following exercise is designed to develop mindfulness of your experience, your interoceptive capacity (the ability to experience the body from within), and more deeply attune to your partner's body. Research shows that interoceptive awareness enhances the sexual experience by decreasing anxiety and self-criticism, while improving mood and present moment awareness. The practice also draws upon beginner's mind as you explore your partner's body with curiosity and an open mind.

Practice: GIVING AND RECEIVING TOUCH

This joint exercise can be done as foreplay or as a standalone exercise and should take about 5 to 10 minutes per partner. However, if one partner is working on decreasing feelings of being overwhelmed during sex, I recommend making this a 5-minute standalone exercise that does not lead to sex. If this is not an issue, make it foreplay, but do not have sex until both partners have been in the receiving role.

1. Choose who will be the giver and who will be the receiver first.

2. Lie side by side, listening to each other's breath, feeling your bodies next to each other. Synchronize your breath with your partner's.

3. Savor the warmth and softness of your partner's body.

4. The giver now touches and explores the receiver's body for 5 to 10 minutes.

5. Both giver and receiver should stay aware of their senses, emotions, physical sensations, and bodily responses. If either partner feels overwhelmed, notices their mind drifting, or starts to shut down, simply let each other know, pause, return to the breath, and slowly resume when you are ready.

6. Move more slowly than you normally would to stay intimately attuned to your partner. Keep sensing what you are feeling as a way to receive physiological feedback about what your partner is experiencing.

7. Just as you would with mindfulness, notice thoughts or distractions, label them, and return your awareness to the breath and touch.

8. When time is up, switch roles.

Variations: 1) If you have sex following this practice, continue noticing and releasing thoughts, slowing down, and returning to the breath and body if you get distracted or feel the urge to pull away. Ask your partner to pause to help you with this process. Once you feel regulated, you can return your attention to your partner. 2) Explore maintaining eye contact during this exercise.

When you have a chance, describe in your journal anything about the experience that you found pleasant, challenging, or surprising.

Intimacy is a dance of togetherness and separateness. When we give of ourselves, we lose our sense of "I" and "you" as separate and distinct entities. It's hard to surrender to this connection when we feel defended or overwhelmed, but by slowing down and being with our body's reactions, we allow ourselves to begin to relax into this feeling of union without losing ourselves.

Wrap-Up

◈ Honesty and vulnerability are essential to intimacy.

◈ Intimacy in our relationship requires us to cultivate safety for our partners through compassion and trust.

◈ Intimacy with others begins with our ability to be intimate with ourselves.

◈ Mindfulness, compassion, and gratitude help soothe and regulate our nervous systems so we can practice greater intimacy.

There's a thread you follow.
It goes among things that change.
But it doesn't change . . .
While you hold it you can't get lost.

—WILLIAM STAFFORD

"THE WAY IT IS"

TEN

Your Road Ahead

CARRYING YOUR NEW PRACTICES FORWARD

Congratulations on all the work you've done to strengthen your relationship! Relating authentically and intimately is arguably the most challenging and rewarding process we face daily. Hopefully you've experienced moments of transformation resulting from your steady practice, commitment, and dedication to facing the difficult stuff and turning toward yourself, your partner, and your relationship. This chapter explores ways you can sustain a shared practice with your partner so that you can continue to experience the benefits of bringing mindfulness, compassion, and gratitude into your relationship for years to come.

I conclude the book with gratitude practices for a reason. One of the easiest, most fun, and most fulfilling ways to keep yourself motivated is to keep expressing your appreciation for your partner and your relationship. However, as mentioned in chapter 8, gratitude's benefits increase with time, so don't get discouraged if you find yourself feeling unappreciative or unappreciated one day. Simply return to the practice of cultivating and expressing gratitude. With continued practice, you will notice feelings of gratitude increasing and flowing more naturally in your relationship.

Remember that habit formation is easier if you create external accountability structures to help you schedule and track your practices. This is essential to making sustainable changes, because mastery of any new skill—including relationship skills—is the result of consistent practice over time. To become masterful at bringing mindfulness into your relationship simply requires repeated practice over the long haul!

Repetition doesn't have to be boring, though; you can vary which practices you emphasize at different times in your relationship to reflect what's going on in your life. What's important is to regularly check in with yourself and your partner to reflect, revise, and reset. I recommend reserving time with your partner for a monthly check-in about the current strengths and challenges in your relationship and what your relationship needs.

In your journal, take a few minutes to reflect on the key takeaways from this book. Perhaps look at the table of contents to jog your memory. Write down the skills and practices you consider most useful. Record any keywords you want to remember about your values. Use this reflection as a blueprint for future check-ins.

Monthly Check-In

Set a monthly check-in date to sit down for 30 to 45 minutes with your partner. Create a calendar reminder so it doesn't slip through the cracks when things get busy. Minimize distractions and plan for your check-in to take place somewhere that reflects the qualities you want to cultivate in your relationship—for instance, if you want to cultivate peacefulness or fun, perhaps choose your living room, a park, or a quiet coffee shop. Plan a nice date or reward afterward, like a bubble bath or a special dinner.

◈ Take 5 minutes to individually review your journal notes, and another 5 minutes to journal individually about how you've done since the last check-in, including:

  ◈ Practices you've kept up with
  ◈ Practices you've abandoned
  ◈ Progress you've noticed
  ◈ Current relationship needs, hopes, and goals
  ◈ Exercises you would like to reintroduce
  ◈ Take 5 minutes each to share what you wrote with your partner.
  ◈ Decide which practices you will commit or recommit to.
  ◈ Together, take a few minutes to review the values and goals you identified in chapter 7. Rewrite your goals as needed.

Do this kind of review and assessment monthly (if monthly feels too frequent, you can choose to do this every other month), and choose which exercises to do based on your relationship needs at the time. If you love certain guided exercises, support your practice by recording them and listen on your smartphone or other device.

STAYING CONNECTED

I didn't write this to be the kind of book you read once then leave on the shelf. This book, and the practices collected here, are intended as an ongoing resource for you and your partner as you move forward in your shared life. Committing—and recommitting—to nurturing your mindful relationship is an ongoing process. Like gently returning your mind to an anchor when you meditate, you may sometimes find that you need to refocus your attention on your joint practices.

In addition to a ritual like the monthly check-in, remember that you can reset and bring your attention back to your mutual goals at any time. Here's a quick reminder of possible ways to stay connected and note your progress through tracking: 1) calendar tracking, 2) journal tracking, and 3) partner check-ins. Revisit the descriptions of these tracking tools in chapter 3 on page 43. Continue to use these tools as your practice together deepens. Your journal provides a good record and reflection tool to help you review and validate your progress moving forward.

An additional tool is "appreciation texting." Express your appreciation for each other via text message throughout the day as a way to help each other feel seen and stay motivated. You can even schedule texts using a text-scheduling app.

Always remember the importance of gratitude! Use journaling, partner check-ins, and texting to express appreciation for any and all progress you see in yourself, your partner, and your relationship. Use your calendar to schedule rewarding couple activities that support your feelings of appreciation for each other and your relationship.

GO DEEPER

Pillow Talk Ritual

You now have some familiarity with the importance of rituals and expressing yourself to your partner, particularly at bedtime. To experience the benefits of a satisfying bedtime ritual, start a "pillow talk" ritual that will keep you reflecting on these practices and engaged in the shared journey toward your relationship values.

You can choose to use a practice from this book as a foundation or design your own ritual based on what you've learned. Make the ritual short and sweet, and include some combination of gratitude, appreciation, mindfulness, and compassion. One idea is to generate "open sentence" statements that will spark meaningful connection and conversation, such as "I feel . . . I need . . . I appreciate . . . I desire . . . I hope . . . I wish . . . I choose . . . I remember . . . I dream of . . . I fear . . . I struggle with . . . I like . . . I'm humbled by . . . I surrender . . ." You could take turns completing one or a few of these statements before bed.

Spend 20 minutes designing a "pillow talk" ritual that would feel nourishing to you as a couple. Discuss obstacles that may get in the way of continuing this ritual (e.g., when you are traveling or apart) and how you will recommit or keep the ritual going if you stop doing it. Write a shared commitment statement (see page 45) in your journals to solidify your new ritual.

LOOKING AHEAD

Congratulations to you both! You've practiced relating to yourself, your partner, and your relationship in new ways. You've experienced detaching from thoughts, noticing your stories, feeling your feelings, discovering and expressing your needs, asking for what you want, resolving conflicts, communicating vulnerably, expressing gratitude, cultivating compassion, and deepening your intimacy through sensory experiences and touch.

You deserve acknowledgment and appreciation, so don't deprive yourselves! You have practiced some pretty aspirational and inspirational foundations for living, loving, and relating in a deeply fulfilling way. Let's conclude this phase of our journey together with one final practice.

Practice: SAVORING

Spend as much time on this solo practice as you would like to. Read the instructions and then place this book aside until you conclude the exercise.

1. Close your eyes and savor this moment. Reflect on the journey you took with your partner that began the moment you decided to read this book together. Remember the collection of moments leading up to now—reading together and separately, practicing the exercises, journaling, and experiencing profound breakthroughs.

2. Let yourself recall all the memories and feelings that arise with them. Cultivate that familiar feeling of gratitude and appreciation. Send that gratitude first toward yourself for all the time, work, energy, and effort you've dedicated to cultivating your relationship. Then send that same gratitude toward your partner.

Recognize that working on your relationship is one of the deepest and most profoundly rewarding investments a person can make.

As you move forward, remember that your relationship is a living, breathing entity that you nurture through growing awareness and deepening practice. Loving well is a choice, a promise, and an act of courage that transcends simple chemistry; to love your partner well entails continual commitment to your values, to each other, and to receiving each other with fresh eyes and an open heart in each moment. The practice of returning again and again to the anchors of each other, your values, and your shared vision and intentions will always illuminate your path forward. In this way, you can still your minds and together set the course of your shared relationship story. In this stillness, you can allow yourself to be desired, seen, and loved . . . and you can give these gifts to your partner as you continue to deepen into the nourishing, supportive, and intimate relationship of your dreams.

Resources

WEBSITES

Brené Brown: www.brenebrown.com

The Center for Nonviolent Communication: www.cnvc.org

Compassion for Couples: www.compassionforcouples.com

Diane Poole Heller, PhD, Somatic Attachment and Trauma Expert: www.dianepooleheller.com

Esther Perel: www.estherperel.com

The Gottman Institute: www.gottman.com

Gratefulness: www.gratefulness.org

Greater Good Science Center: ggsc.berkeley.edu

HeartMath: www.heartmath.com

The International Focusing Institute: www.focusing.org

PREPARE/ENRICH: www.prepare-enrich.com

Stan Tatkin Psychobiological Approach to Couple Therapy: www.stantatkin.com

Sue Johnson, PhD: "What Is EFT?": www.drsuejohnson.com/emotionally-focused-therapy-2/what-is-eft/

Tara Brach: www.tarabrach.com

BOOKS

Awakening the Heart: A Somatic Training in Bodhicitta (Audible Course) by Reginald A. Ray, PhD (Sounds True, 2017)

The Five-Minute Journal: A Happier You in 5 Minutes a Day by Intelligent Change (Intelligent Change Inc., 2013)

Get Out of Your Mind and Into Your Life: The New Acceptance and Commitment Therapy by Steven C. Hayes, PhD, with Spencer Smith (New Harbinger Publications, 2005)

The Highly Sensitive Person in Love: Understanding and Managing Relationships When the World Overwhelms You by Elaine N. Aron, PhD (Harmony Books, 2001)

Hold Me Tight: Conversations for a Lifetime of Love by Dr. Sue Johnson (Little, Brown and Company, 2008)

How Can I Get Through to You?: Closing the Intimacy Gap Between Men and Women by Terrence Real (Fireside, 2002)

How to Be an Adult in Relationships: The Five Keys to Mindful Loving by David Richo (Shambhala Publications, Inc., 2002)

If the Buddha Dated: A Handbook for Finding Love on a Spiritual Path by Charlotte Kasl, PhD (Penguin Books, 1999)

If the Buddha Married: Creating Enduring Relationships on a Spiritual Path by Charlotte Kasl, PhD (Penguin Books, 2001)

Intimate Communion: Awakening Your Sexual Essence by David Deida (Health Communications Inc., 1995)

Inward by Yung Pueblo (Andrews McMeel Publishing, 2018)

Mating in Captivity: Unlocking Erotic Intelligence by Esther Perel (Harper, 2017)

Mindful Relationship Habits: 25 Practices for Couples to Enhance Intimacy, Nurture Closeness, and Grow a Deeper Connection by S. J. Scott and Barrie Davenport (Oldtown Publishing LLC, 2017)

The Mindful Self-Compassion Workbook: A Proven Way to Accept Yourself, Build Inner Strength, and Thrive by Kristin Neff, PhD, and Christopher Germer, PhD (The Guilford Press, 2018)

Passionate Marriage: Keeping Love and Intimacy Alive in Committed Relationships by David Schnarch, PhD (W. W. Norton and Company, 2009)

Perfect Love, Imperfect Relationships: Healing the Wound of the Heart by John Welwood (Trumpeter, 2007)

The Places that Scare You: A Guide to Fearlessness in Difficult Times by Pema Chodron (Shambhala Publications, Inc., 2002)

Radical Acceptance: Embracing Your Life with the Heart of a Buddha by Tara Brach, PhD (Bantam Dell, 2003)

Real Love: The Art of Mindful Connection by Sharon Salzberg (Flatiron Books, 2017)

True Love: A Practice for Awakening the Heart by Thich Nhat Hanh (Shambhala Publications, Inc., 2006)

Wired for Love: How Understanding Your Partner's Brain and Attachment Style Can Help You Defuse Conflict and Build a Secure Relationship by Stan Tatkin, PsyD (New Harbinger Publications, 2012)

The Wisdom of a Broken Heart: How to Turn the Pain of a Breakup into Healing, Insight, and New Love by Susan Piver (Atria Paperback, 2010)

APPS

Calm

Couple

Five Minute Journal

Gottman Card Decks

Headspace

Insight Timer – Meditation

Journey LIVE Group Meditation (Apple)

Kindu For Couples

Moodnotes

Exercises

CHAPTER ONE

Practice: Breath Awareness
Practice: A Mindful Meal
Practice: Body Scan
Practice: Cultivating Beginner's Mind
Practice: Attuning to Our Partners (or "Bae Meditation")
Go Deeper: Reflecting on Attunement
Practice: Heart Meditation
Practice: Plan a Mindful Date

CHAPTER TWO

Practice: Leaves on a Stream Meditation
Practice: Yes-No
Go Deeper: Your Best Life
Practice: My Self-Stories
Practice: My Partner Stories
Practice: Love Languages
Practice: Strength and Growth Areas
Practice: Meeting Each Other as We Are

CHAPTER THREE

Go Deeper: Create Your Weekly Practice Schedule

CHAPTER FOUR

Go Deeper: Evaluations Versus Observations
Practice: RAIN
Practice: RAINing on Your Inner Critic's Parade
Practice: Heart Talks
Practice: Forgiveness
Practice: RAINing on Relationship Dynamics
Practice: Behavioral Chain Analysis

CHAPTER FIVE

Practice: Noticing Thoughts and Feelings
Practice: Expansion
Practice: Focusing
Practice: Soften, Soothe, Allow
Go Deeper: Naming Your Emotions
Practice: Eyes On
Practice: Perspective-Taking Through Assertiveness and Active Listening

CHAPTER SIX

Practice: Needs Versus Preferences
Go Deeper: Feelings and Needs List
Practice: Identifying My Needs
Practice: Identifying Deeper Patterns
Practice: Hugging till Relaxed
Practice: Underneath Anger Meditation
Practice: Putting It All Together
Practice: Asking Without Attachment

CHAPTER SEVEN

Go Deeper: Create Your Weekly Practice Schedule

CHAPTER EIGHT

Practice: Gratitude Drop-In
Practice: The Gratitude Bias
Practice: Picture Memories
Practice: Daily Gratitude Journal
Practice: Gratitude Love Lists
Go Deeper: Shared Gratitude List
Practice: Self-Appreciation
Practice: Gestures of Appreciation
Practice: Dutch Wine Box Tradition

CHAPTER NINE

CHAPTER TEN

References

INTRODUCTION

Doubek, James, and NPR Staff. "Attention, Students: Put Your Laptops Away." *National Public Radio.* April 17, 2016. Accessed June 25, 2019. https://www.npr.org/2016/04/17/474525392/attention-students-put-your-laptops-away.

"Esther Perel | Modern Love and Relationships | SXSW 2018" YouTube video, 55:12, "SXSW," March 9, 2018. https://www.youtube.com/watch?v=5iu9_8Vsmtk.

Kasl, Charlotte. If the Buddha Married: Creating Enduring Relationships on a Spiritual Path. New York: Penguin Books, 2001.

Mejia, Zameena. "Harvard's Longest Study of Adult Life Reveals How You Can Be Happier and More Successful." *CNBC Make It.* October 31, 2017. Accessed June 25, 2019. https://www.cnbc.com/2017/10/31/this-harvard-study-reveals-how-you-can-be-happier-and-more-successful.html.

CHAPTER ONE

Ackerman, Courtney. "23 Amazing Health Benefits of Mindfulness for Body and Brain." *Positive Psychology.* June 3, 2017. Accessed June 25, 2019. http://www.positivepsychologyprogram.com/benefits-of-mindfulness/.

Brewer, Judson A., Kathleen A. Garrison, and Susan Whitfield-Gabrieli. "What About the 'Self' is Processed in the Posterior Cingulate Cortex?" *Frontiers in Human Neuroscience 7* (October 2013): 647. doi:10.3389/fnhum.2013.00647.

Bureau of Labor Statistics. "Economic News Release: Table 2. Time Spent in Primary Activities and Percent of the Civilian Population Engaging in Each Activity, Averages Per Day on Weekdays and Weekends, 2018 Annual Averages." Updated June 19, 2019. Accessed June 25, 2019. United States Department of Labor. http://www.bls.gov/news.release/atus.t02.htm.

Fromm, Erich. The Art of Loving. Introduction by Peter D. Kramer. New York: Harper Perennial Modern Classics, 2006.

Hamrick, Karen, David Hopkins, and Ket McClelland. "How Much Time Do Americans Spend Eating?" *The Free Library.* December 1, 2008. Accessed June 25, 2019. http://www.thefreelibrary.com/How+much+time+do+Americans+spend+eating%3F-a0190462486.

Harris, Russ. The Happiness Trap How to Stop Struggling and Start Living. Boston, MA: Trumpeter Books, 2008.

Harvard Health Letter. "Mindful Eating." *Harvard Health Publishing*. February 2011. Accessed June 25, 2019. http://www.health.harvard.edu/staying-healthy/mindful-eating.

Hasenkamp, Wendy, Christine D. Wilson-Mendenhall, Erica Duncan, and Lawrence W. Barsalou. "Mind Wandering and Attention During Focused Meditation: A Fine-Grained Temporal Analysis of Fluctuating Cognitive States." *NeuroImage* 59, no. 1 (January 2011): 750–760. doi:10.1016/j.neuroimage.2011.07.008.

HeartMath. "The Science of HeartMath." Accessed June 25, 2019. http://www.heartmath.com/science/.

Hendershot, Carol. "Thing Called Mindfulness." Grand Rapids Center for Mindfulness. Accessed June 25, 2019. http://www.grandrapidscenterformindfulness.com/thing-called-mindfulness/.

Janssen, Lieneke K., Iris Duif, Ilke van Loon, Jeanne H. M. de Vries, Anne E. M. Speckens, Roshan Cools, and Esther Aarts. "Greater Mindful Eating Practice Is Associated with Better Reversal Learning." *Scientific Reports* 8 (April 2018): 5702. doi:10.1038/s41598-018-24001-1.

Kasl, Charlotte. If the Buddha Dated: *A Handbook for Finding Love on a Spiritual Path.* New York: Penguin Books, 1999.

Killingsworth, Matthew A., and Daniel T. Gilbert. "A Wandering Mind Is an Unhappy Mind." *Science* 330, no. 6006 (November 2010): 932. doi:10.1126/science.1192439.

Neff, Kristin, and Christopher Germer. The Mindful Self-Compassion Workbook: *A Proven Way to Accept Yourself, Build Inner Strength, and Thrive.* New York and London: The Guilford Press, 2018.

Taylor, Véronique A., Véronique Daneault, Joshua Grant, Genevievè Scavone, Estelle Breton, Sébastien Roffe-Vidal, and Jérôme Courtemanche, et al. "Impact of Meditation Training on the Default Mode Network During a Restful State." *Social Cognitive and Affective Neuroscience* 8, no. 1 (January 2013): 4–14. doi:10.1093/scan/nsr087.

CHAPTER TWO

Brown, Brené. *The Gifts of Imperfection: Let Go of Who You Think You're Supposed to Be and Embrace Who You Are.* Center City, MN: Hazelden, 2010.

Chapman, Gary. *The Five Love Languages: The Secret to Love that Lasts.* Chicago: Northfield Publishing, 1992.

Lev, Avigail, and Matthew McKay. *Acceptance and Commitment Therapy for Couples: A Clinician's Guide to Using Mindfulness, Values, and Schema Awareness to Rebuild Relationships*. Oakland, CA: Context Press, 2017.

CHAPTER THREE

Durant, Will. *The Story of Philosophy*. New York: Simon & Schuster: 1926.

Hayes, Steven. "The Six Core Processes of ACT." *Association for Contextual Behavioral Science*. Accessed June 25, 2019. http://www.contextualscience.org/the_six_core_processes_of_act.

Intelligent Change. *The Five-Minute Journal*. Toronto, Canada: Intelligent Change, Inc., 2016.

Lally, Phillipa, Cornelia H. M. van Jaarsveld, Henry W. W. Potts, and Jane Wardle. "How Are Habits Formed: Modelling Habit Formation in the Real World." *European Journal of Social Psychology* 40, no. 6 (October 2010): 998–1009. doi:10.1002/ejsp.674.

Psychology Discussion. "Habit Formation: Basis, Types and Measures for Effective Habit Formation." Accessed June 25, 2019. http://www.psychologydiscussion.net/habits/habit-formation-basis-types-and-measures-for-effective-habit-formation/638.

Pychyl, Timothy A. "Goal Progress and Happiness: How to Decrease Procrastination and Increase Happiness." *Psychology Today*. June 7, 2008. Accessed June 25, 2019. http://www.psychologytoday.com/us/blog/dont-delay/200806/goal-progress-and-happiness.

PART TWO

Lavner, Justin A., and Thomas N. Bradbury. "Why Do Even Satisfied Newlyweds Eventually Go on to Divorce?" *Journal of Family Psychology* 26, no. 1 (2012): 1–10. doi:10.1037/a0025966.

Werrbach, Maureen. "Predicting Divorce: The Four Horsemen of the Apocalypse." *Psych Central*. Updated July 8, 2018. Accessed June 25, 2019. http://www.psychcentral.com/blog/predicting-divorce-the-four-horsemen-of-the-apocalpyse/.

CHAPTER FOUR

Lev, Avigail, and Matthew McKay. *Acceptance and Commitment Therapy for Couples: A Clinician's Guide to Using Mindfulness, Values, and Schema Awareness to Rebuild Relationships*. Oakland, CA: Context Press, 2017.

Neff, Kristin, and Christopher Germer. *The Mindful Self-Compassion Workbook: A Proven Way to Accept Yourself, Build Inner Strength, and Thrive.* New York and London: The Guilford Press, 2018.

Rosenberg, Marshall B. *Nonviolent Communication: A Language of Life.* Encinitas, CA: PuddleDancer Press, 2003.

CHAPTER FIVE

Bahrami, Shrein H. *Stop Bingeing, Start Living: Proven Therapeutic Strategies for Breaking the Binge Eating Cycle.* Emeryville, CA: Althea Press, 2018.

Hooks, Bell. *All About Love: New Visions.* New York: William Morrow and Company, 2000.

PREPARE/ENRICH Workbook for Couples. Roseville, MN: PREPARE/ENRICH, 2008, 2015, 2017.

Verduyn, Philippe, and Saskia Lavrijsen. "Which Emotions Last Longest and Why: The Role of Event Importance and Rumination." *Motivation and Emotion* 39, no. 1 (February 2015): 119–127. doi:10.1007/s11031-014-9445-y.

Young, Karen. "The Longest Lasting Emotion and 4 Proven Ways to Loosen its Grip." *Hey Sigmund.* Accessed June 25, 2019. http://www.heysigmund.com/which-emotion-lasts-longer-than-any-other/.

CHAPTER SIX

Richo, David. *How to Be an Adult in Relationships: The Five Keys to Mindful Loving.* Boulder, CO: Shambhala Publications, Inc., 2002.

The Right Words and Beyond. "The NVC Model: Step 4, Requests." Accessed June 25, 2019. http://www.therightword.info/nvc/needs-based-communication/requests/.

The Right Words and Beyond. "The Connection Request." Accessed June 25, 2019. http://www.therightword.info/nvc/needs-based-communication/connection-request/.

Rosenberg, Marshall B. *Nonviolent Communication: A Language of Life.* Encinitas, CA: PuddleDancer Press, 2003.

Schnarch, David. *Passionate Marriage: Keeping Love and Intimacy Alive in Committed Relationships.* New York: W. W. Norton and Company, 2009.

CHAPTER SEVEN

Deci, Edward L., with Richard Flaste. *Why We Do What We Do: Understanding Self-Motivation.* London: Penguin Books, 1996.

Psychology Discussion. "Habit Formation: Basis, Types and Measures for Effective Habit Formation." Accessed June 25, 2019. http://www.psychologydiscussion.net /habits/habit-formation-basis-types-and-measures-for-effective-habit -formation/638.

Pychyl, Timothy A. "Goal Progress and Happiness: How to Decrease Pro-crastination and Increase Happiness." *Psychology Today.* June 7, 2008. Accessed June 25, 2019. http://www.psychologytoday.com/us/blog/dont-delay/200806 /goal-progress-and-happiness.

PART THREE

Emmons, Robert A., and Michael McCullough. "Counting Blessings versus Burdens: An Experimental Investigation of Gratitude and Subjective Well-Being in Daily Life." *Journal of Personality and Social Psychology* 84, no. 2 (February 2003): 377–389. doi:10.1037/0022-3514.84.2.377.

Intelligent Change. *The Five-Minute Journal.* Toronto, Canada: Intelligent Change, Inc., 2016.

Zahn, Roland, Jorge Moll, Mirella Paiva, Griselda Garrido, Frank Krueger, Edward D. Huey, and Jordan Grafman. "The Neural Basis of Human Social Values: Evidence from Functional MRI." *Cerebral Cortex* 19, no. 2 (February 2009):276–83. doi:10.1093/cercor/bhn080.

CHAPTER EIGHT

Algoe, Sara B., Shelly L. Gable, and Natalya C. Maisel. "It's the Little Things: Everyday Gratitude as a Booster Shot for Romantic Relationships." *Personal Relationships* 17, issue 2 (June 2010): 217–233. doi:10.1111/j.1475-6811 .2010.01273.x.

Craig, Heather. "The Research on Gratitude and Its Link with Love and Happi-ness." *Positive Psychology.* March 3, 2019. Accessed June 25, 2019. http://www .positivepsychologyprogram.com/gratitude-research/.

Emmons, Robert A., and Michael McCullough. "Counting Blessings versus Burdens: An Experimental Investigation of Gratitude and Subjective Well-Being in Daily Life." *Journal of Personality and Social Psychology* 84, no. 2 (February 2003): 377–389. doi:10.1037/0022-3514.84.2.377.

Gottman, John, and Julie Gottman. "The Natural Principles of Love." *Journal of Family Theory & Review* 9, issue 1 (March 2017): 7–26. doi:10.1111/jftr.12182.

Intelligent Change. *The Five-Minute Journal.* Toronto, Canada: Intelligent Change, Inc., 2016.

Kasl, Charlotte. *If the Buddha Dated: A Handbook for Finding Love on a Spiritual Path.* New York: Penguin Books, 1999.

Kindt, Sara, Maarten Vansteenkiste, Annmarie Cano, and Liesbet Goubert. "When Is Your Partner Willing to Help You? The Role of Daily Goal Conflict and Perceived Gratitude." *Motivation and Emotion* 41, no. 6 (December 2017): 671–82. doi:10.1007/s11031-017-9635-5.

Lambert, Nathaniel M., Margaret S. Clark, Jared Durtschi, Frank D. Fincham, and Steven M. Graham. "Benefits of Expressing Gratitude: Expressing Gratitude to a Partner Changes One's View of the Relationship." *Psychological Science* 21, no. 4 (April 2010). 574–580. doi:10.1177/0956797610364003.

Neff, Kristin, and Christopher Germer. *The Mindful Self-Compassion Workbook: A Proven Way to Accept Yourself, Build Inner Strength, and Thrive.* New York and London: The Guilford Press, 2018.

Restrepo, Sandra, dir. *Brené Brown: The Call to Courage.* Netflix, 2019. http://www.netflix.com/title/81010166.

Suttie, Jill. "Can Gratitude Help Couples Through Hard Times?" *Greater Good Magazine.* May 24, 2018. Accessed June 25, 2019. http://greatergood.berkeley .edu/article/item/can_gratitude_help_couples_through_hard_times.

Vincent, Emily. "Writing Power: Kent State Professor Studies Benefits of Writing Gratitude Letters." *Kent State University.* Accessed July 3, 2019. http://einside .kent.edu/Management%20Update%20Archive/news/announcements/success /toepferwriting.html.

Wong, Joel, and Joshua Brown. "How Gratitude Changes You and Your Brain: New Research Is Starting to Explore How Gratitude Works to Improve Our Mental Health." *Greater Good Magazine.* June 6, 2017. Accessed June 25, 2019. http://greatergood.berkeley.edu/article/item/how_gratitude_changes_you _and_your_brain.

Wood, Alex M., Jeffrey J. Froh, and Adam A. Geraghty. "Gratitude and Well-Being: A Review and Theoretical Integration." *Clinical Psychology Review* 30, no. 7 (November 2010): 890–905. doi:10.1016/j.cpr.2010.03.005.

Zahn, Roland, Jorge Moll, Mirella Paiva, Griselda Garrido, Frank Krueger, Edward D. Huey, and Jordan Grafman. "The Neural Basis of Human Social Values: Evidence from Functional MRI." *Cerebral Cortex* 19, no. 2 (February 2009): 276–83. doi:10.1093/cercor/bhn080.

CHAPTER NINE

Chambers, Richard and Margie Ulbrick. *Mindful Relationships: Creating Genuine Connections with Ourselves and Others.* Wollombi, Australia: Exisle Publishing, 2016.

Hanh, Thich Nhat. *True Love: A Practice for Awakening the Heart.* Boulder, CO: Shambhala Publications, Inc., 2006.

Kasl, Charlotte. *If the Buddha Dated: A Handbook for Finding Love on a Spiritual Path.* New York: Penguin Books, 1999.

Leigh, Jasmine. "Pillow Talk: Find Out What She Wants to Hear Right After Sex." *AskMen.* Accessed June 25, 2019. http://www.askmen.com/dating/love_tip _300/392_love_tip.html.

Neff, Kristin, and S. Natasha Beretvas. "The Role of Self-Compassion in Romantic Relationships." *Self and Identity* 12, issue 1 (2013): 78–98. doi:10.1080/15298 868.2011.639548.

Sadhegi, Habib. *Within: A Spiritual Awakening to Love & Weight Loss.* New York: Open Road Media, 2014.

Seppälä, Emma M. "The Real Secret to Intimacy (and Why It Scares Us)." *Psychology Today.* September 5, 2012. Accessed June 25, 2019. http://www .psychologytoday.com/us/blog/feeling-it/201209/the-real-secret-intimacy -and-why-it-scares-us.

Smith, Briallyn. "12 Things Happy Couples Talk About and Feel Closer!" *Love-Panky.* Accessed June 25, 2019. http://www.lovepanky.com/love-couch /romantic-love/12-things-happy-couples-talk-about-and-feel-closer.

Weisman, Sige. "How to Create a Couple Bubble in Your Relationship." *SFWT Therapy for Women & Couples Counseling.* November 6, 2017. Accessed June 25, 2019. http://www.sfwomenstherapy.com/couples-counseling /create-couple-bubble-relationship/.

CHAPTER TEN

Flint, Jessica. "Desire Cards." In The School of Recovery.

Stafford, William. "The Way It Is." *In The Way It Is: New and Selected Poems.* Minneapolis, MN: Graywolf Press, 1998.

Suttie, Jill. "Can Gratitude Help Couples Through Hard Times?" *Greater Good Magazine.* May 24, 2018. Accessed June 25, 2019. http://greatergood.berkeley .edu/article/item/can_gratitude_help_couples_through_hard_times.

Index

Focusing, 75–76
Forgiveness, 62–64, 68

G
Germer, Christopher, 63, 76,
    93–94, 128
Goal-setting, 43–45, 103–104
Gratitude
    benefits of, 111, 113–116, 145
    everyday practice, 116–118, 125
    present moment awareness
        of, 115
    self-appreciation, 121
    for your partner, 118–120
    for your relationship, 122–124

H
Habit-building, 41–43,
    101–102, 145–146
Heart meditation, 17–18
Heart talks, 61–62
hooks, bell, 70
Hugging, 92–93
Humor, 25

I
Inner critic, 59–60
Intimacy, 110–111, 127
    emotional, 134–138
    physical, 139–142
    with yourself, 131–134, 143

J
Journal tracking, 43

K
Kasl, Charlotte, xii, 4, 112, 126
Krishnamurti, Jiddu, 54

L
Leaves on a stream
    meditation, 25
Love languages, 32–33
Love mantras, 136–138

M
Mantras, 136–138
Mindful eating, 7–8
Mindfulness, benefits of, 5–6
Mindful Self-Compassion Work-
    book, The (Neff and Germer),
    63, 76, 93–94
Mindful sex, 139

N
Needs
    feelings and, 86–87
    identifying your, 88–91
    making and receiving requests,
        95–97
    vs. preferences, 85–86
    your partner's, 91–94
Neff, Kristin, 63, 76, 93–94, 128
Negativity bias, 113
Nhat Hanh, Thich, 136
"No," freedom to say, 97–98, 134
Nonviolent Communication (NVC)
    model, 53

O
Observations
    about your partner, 60–64
    about your relationship, 64–68
    about yourself, 58–60
    vs. evaluations, 55–57, 68

P
Partner check-ins, 43

Acknowledgments

Writing this book has been transformational for me. Thank you to Callisto Media and Katie Parr for this opportunity and to my editors, Camille Hayes, Carol Rosenberg, and Claire Yee, for their support and guidance.

I want to express immense gratitude to Shrein Bahrami, LMFT, and Seth Sherman, MD, for their generosity, support, insight, and editing.

Thank you to my colleagues who supported me in ways visible and invisible during this journey: Trina Brown, Avigail Lev, Jessica Harvey, Abbie Zimmerman, Drew Anne Wolfson, Kristel Grodeska, Adriana Albano, Naveen Kassamali, Lindsay Goodlin, Adriana Popescu, Forrest Franken, and Kerstin Marie Wheale.

Appreciation to Stephen Burnett for his fabulous improv facilitation skills, humor, and inspiration.

Heartfelt gratitude to my family and friends, near and far: Rebecca Farrar, Jon Glancy, Adriana Cerundolo, Emilie Schattman, Emily Fox-Kessler, Vidya Kaipa and Alex Grande, Adam Hundt, Robin Gruver, Chelsea Kirby and Nick Johnson Lee, Emily Gutierrez, Cara Kinkel, Regan Parrish, Mark Korshak, Joanna Korshak, the Cathey Family, Elia and Jordan Infascelli-Smith, Tory and Chris Bagdasarian, Nancy Birdwell, Whitney Birdwell, and Brooke and Randy Ferguson.

Special thanks to Rachael and Indy.

About the Author

Lauren Korshak, LMFT, is a San Francisco-based marriage and family therapist and meditation teacher. In her private practice, classes, workshops, and groups, Lauren helps individuals and couples transform their love lives through heart-centered mindfulness. For nearly a decade, Lauren has provided counseling in a variety of settings to individuals and couples looking to improve their relationships, careers, and mental health. Lauren has contributed to articles featured in *PopSugar, Elephant Journal, Martha Stewart Weddings,* and *Wedding Wire.*